INSIGHT POCKET GUIDE

CORSICA

APA PUBLICATIONS

Part of the Langenscheidt Publishing Group

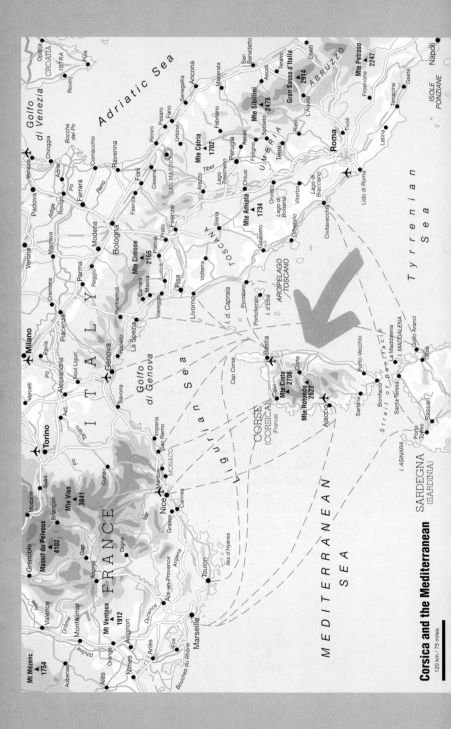

Corsica and the Mediterranean

120 km / 75 miles

Welcome!

This guidebook combines the interests and enthusiasms of two of the world's best-known information providers: Insight Guides, who have set the standard for visual travel guides since 1970, and Discovery Channel, the world's premier source of non-fiction television programming.

In these pages Insight Guides' correspondent on Corsica, Alphons Schauseil, brings you the best of the island in 14 day itineraries based in and around the island's main centres of Bastia, an Italian-flavoured town in the northeast which is well-placed for a tour of Cap Corse; Corte, in the centre (and a springboard for some of Corsica's most interesting mountain villages); Bonifacio, in the south; and Calvi, in the northwest. These carefully crafted itineraries include detailed directions for getting around and recommended restaurants to try en route. They are designed to help visitiors experience the island's many and varied aspects, especially its natural beauty and rich culture rooted in Greek, Byzantine, Italian and French influences.

Alphons Schauseil lives in a Corsican village overlooking the ocean. Returning home from abroad, he gets the same thrill as he did on his first visit. What he loves about Corsica is not just the stunning scenery – soaring peaks, dramatic coastline and remote mountain villages – but the people, whose distinct 'Corsitude' always makes an impression. **David Abram,** the updater of this edition, is a renowned expert on trekking in Corsica.

C O N T E N T S

*Pages 2/3:
mountain
eyrie*

*Pages 8/9:
Bonifacio's
dramatic
port of entry*

HISTORY &

Corsica's first ever tourist arrived by sea 3,300 years ago. The Greek hero Odysseus landed here once the gods had sent him off on his wanderings after the fall of Troy. Homer describes how Odysseus ended up 'in a narrow fjord protected by an unbroken wall of rock' – the harbour in question is thought to be that of Bonifacio. He didn't get much of a welcome: the huge denizens of the island, the Laestrygons, threw huge boulders down on him and his men, forcing them to beat a hasty retreat. These Bronze Age inhabitants do indeed seem to have had almost Cyclopean strength. Their stone forts, mostly round structures called *torre*, were built out of piles of incredibly heavy stone slabs on sites with commanding views. The historians have thus named these people the Torréens.

They weren't the original inhabitants of the island, however. Their predecessors, the Neolithic Corsi, appear to have been peaceful shep-

Vestige of the island's prehistoric past at Fontanaccia

Culture

The Romans left their mark as well

herds and hunters. From 4,000BC onwards, though, they seem to have felt themselves increasingly under threat, and began building *castelli* by adding walls to natural rock formations to make defensive forts. They were also the first people in Western civilisation to create life-sized as well as oversized human sculptures. The Torréens and the Corsi must have fused together at some stage to create a people whose actual habitat was the relatively inaccessible mountain regions of the island. Here they retreated to escape the other conquerors who were arriving from across the seas.

Antiquity and Christianity

Around the year 565BC Phocaean Greeks arrived on Corsica, at the mouth of the Tavignanu on the east coast, and founded the trading town of Alalia. They subjugated the Corsicans who lived nearby, forced them to clear the surrounding plains of vegetation, and then had them plant grain, vineyards and olive trees. They also mined ore deposits in the nearby hills, but did not venture any further into the mountains. The Greek historian Diodorus is full of praise for the social system of the Corsi, seeing them as practising 'justice under all conditions of life'.

Greek hegemony lasted for three centuries; after a brief Carthaginian interlude they were finally expelled by the Romans in 259BC. The new conquerors turned Alalia into Aléria and used legion veterans to found a second town, Mariana, on the estuary of the Golu, and several smaller bases all around the island. However, it was only when the Romans' ancient gods were replaced by Christianity that they began to have any influence on the majority of the islanders. A first basilica was built in Mariana towards the end of the 4th century, and the Latin language made its way into even the remotest valleys to become a fundamental element of the Corsican language.

After the collapse of the Roman Empire around AD456, the Vandals repeatedly sacked the island for nearly 80 years until they were finally driven off for good in 534 by the troops of Byzantine Emperor Justinian I. The new lords of the island turned out to be just as repressive and cruel, however; Pope Gregory the Great was finally forced to intervene in order to keep Christianity on the island. In 774 the King of the Franks and the Lombards, later Emperor Charlemagne, presented the island to the Vatican as a gift.

The 9th-century chapel of Santa Reparata

Ever since the year 700, though, more and more strange sails had been appearing on the horizon. The Moors, or Saracens, of northern Africa had terrorised the Mediterranean coastline for centuries – and the people of Corsica, bled dry by previous invasions, were scarcely able to put up any resistance. Charlemagne rushed to the island's aid in 806 and at first managed to beat the Moors, but in the fierce fighting the Corsicans lost 90 percent of their men. However, the Tuscan Count Bonifacio chased the Saracens all the way back to their homeland, and on his return he built a citadel on the southern tip of the island, naming it after himself. But after his death the Moors returned and also set up fortifications, forcing thousands of islanders to flee to Italy.

It was only in 1016 that the Moors were driven off the island by Genoese and Pisan forces. They left a devastated land behind them, and also the anopheles mosquito.

It wasn't until after World War II that these fertile strips of land were sprayed free of malaria once and for all. The Moorish epoch, however, altered the face of Corsica and its traces still remain to this day. The constant threat made the island's population withdraw to the mountains, and until recent times they built their villages in relatively inaccessible places, high up in the foothills with commanding views, and always on the lookout for strangers. The coastal strips were nothing more than *piaghja*, or pastureland, to them.

Pisans and Genoese

Settlement along the coast began with the construction of fortified bases by the Genoese and the Pisans between the 13th and 15th centuries. Ever since the defeat of the Moors the two city-republics had been squabbling over the right to administer and exploit the Vaticanowned island. In 1091, a Pope assigned this right to Pisa. Two centuries of peace followed, during which the finest churches on the island were built. The Pisan administrators grew rich and introduced a feudal system, appointing themselves counts and barons. But then Genoa, which had maintained its coastal fortresses, delivered a crushing blow to the fleet of its rival, Pisa, at the Battle of Lepanto in 1284. At a stroke, all the island's riches now belonged to the Genoese.

At first, however, Genoa had to fight things out with the King of Aragon, whom the Vatican had placed in charge of the island. The South Corsican count Vincentellu d'Istria allied himself with the House of Aragon, subjugated almost the entire island with the exception of Bonifacio and Calvi, founded the Citadel of Corte in the island's interior in 1419, and was finally appointed a Viceroy by the Spaniards. He incurred the islanders' wrath, however, when he raised taxes; the Genoese caught him while he was trying to escape and beheaded him.

To defeat the island's feudal lords *(signori)*, Genoa made a pact with the Corsicans in 1359; it assured them protection and a proper system of justice in return for lower taxation. An uprising against the regime led to agricultural reform; north of the central mountain chain, ownership of fertile land was transferred to local parishes. In around 1370 these joined together to form larger units known as *pievi*, governed by *capurali*, whose job it was to represent Corsican interests to the Genoese. As time went on, however, these *capurali* succeeded in promoting themselves to the rank of new lords of the island and ended up embroiled in a power struggle with the *Signori* from the southern part of the island. The ensuing civil war made the island completely ungovernable as far as the Genoese were concerned.

In 1453 the city-republic of Genoa, discouraged, ceded administration of the island to the Genoese private Bank of St George, which could afford its own army. This bank installed a unique early-warning system to thwart attacks on the island by Moorish pirates, which were still posing a problem: they had nearly 200 towers built along the coast that could provide fire and smoke signals from their battlements. The Corsicans had to do all this work and finance it too, and this also applied to highway and bridge construction. More and more Genoese settlers moved to the island. Despotism became the order of the day, the justice system became utterly corrupt, and mob law claimed thousands of lives, until, in 1729, a new tax sparked off a general uprising against the Genoese.

Pope Boniface VIII

King Theodore coin

The Corsican Fight for Freedom

The Corsican militia finally gained the upper hand. In 1735, a *consulta* proclaimed an island kingdom – but one without a monarch. When, one year later, the Westphalian idealist and adventurer Baron Theodor von Neuhof arrived on the island near Aléria and promised the Corsicans help from abroad, he was instantly proclaimed King Theodore I. The intrigues of the great powers, however, were to prove his undoing. In 1737 a contingent of French troops landed on the island to win back Corsica for Genoa, in return for a large sum of money. The Corsicans were forced to bow to French might, and their ringleaders went into exile. Until 1753 it remained uncertain who actually controlled the island: France, Genoa or the Corsicans themselves. In 1751, a *consulta* passed the island's own constitution and appointed the worthy General Gaffori as head of government. Genoa murdered him.

His successor was Pasquale Paoli, aged just over 30, whose father had also been Regent under Theodore I for a time. The young man, who had studied during his exile in Italy, succeeded in transforming Corsica into a unified state within just a few years. Soon, only the fortified coastal towns still belonged to the Genoese. Paoli created a new justice system that was free of bribery, under which every vendetta killing was severely punished, and this gradually fostered an atmosphere of trust. He divided Corsica up into nine major regions, with Corte as their capital. Under a new constitution, one member of the parliament could be voted for by groups of 1,000 inhabitants respectively, and would then receive one seat and one vote in the *consulta* of Corte. This national parliament was strengthened by a good balance between political and legal responsibility. Paoli actively encouraged education and industry, had some coins minted and created a national army out of the rural militia. His democratic ideas were a model for the founding fathers of the United States and the ideologues of the French Revolution.

However, absolutism and cold power politics still dominated the mainland. In 1768 Genoa empowered the King of France to win back Corsica and rule there as Regent, and offered him the sum of two million pounds for his pains. Even though Louis XV knew full well that such a sum could never be raised, the invasion began. Early on in the fighting, a French expeditionary force was crushingly defeated by the Corsicans near Borgu, but soon there were more than 30,000 French troops on the island. The decisive battle took place in May 1769 on the bridge over the Golo near Ponte

Pasquale Paoli, Corsica's greatest hero

Nuevo. The superior force of the enemy finally sealed the fate of the young Corsican nation. Paoli was forced to flee to England.

The French army crushed the last vestiges of resistance with appalling brutality. Members of the nobility who supported France were awarded titles and grants to educate their children at French schools. One favoured cadet was Napoleon Bonaparte, born in the same year the nation was defeated. As Emperor he ruled the French and embroiled Europe in war. But he did very little for his native island.

The outbreak of the French Revolution seemed to provide the Corsicans with one more chance for self-determination. Paoli returned from exile in 1790, and was celebrated as a freedom-fighter even in Paris. But because he tried to keep Corsica out of the confusion and horror of the revolutionary years, the Parisian revolutionaries declared him a traitor to his country. Paoli was forced to flee yet again, and

Napoleon Bonaparte

died in exile in London in 1807. The Corsicans made more attempts to fight the French, and real calm only descended on the island in 1816 when France forgot about Corsica.

Decline and Tourism

As recently as 1911, it was still only possible to reach 300 out of Corsica's 400 or so villages via mule tracks. During World War I, however, the Corsicans suddenly became important. The price they paid was high, though: at least 30,000 men 'fell for France'. The culture that had been built up by several generations gradually became obliterated. During World War II the island was occupied by fascist Italy, but fighting only actually began in 1943 when German troops withdrew to Corsica from Sardinia. In October that year, Corsica was the first French territory to be liberated. After the war, however, it only seemed possible to make a living either on the Italian mainland or in the colonies. Between 1936 and 1960, the island's population dwindled by half; whole villages were abandoned.

In 1957 the government in Paris decided to cultivate the land once again, and to use the island as a source of income from tourism. Settlers – some of them of Corsican origin – returning from the various parts of North Africa that had recently won their independence, created their own monocultures with the aid of state subsidies, and the island's own smallholders had no chance to compete against these newcomers. At the same time, tourist development of the beaches drew the last of the island's young people away from the villages in the interior. This resulted in despair, indignation and finally open protest.

In 1966 the first 'regionalistic' movement was formed, which went on to espouse Paoli's ideas under various different names and became a militant 'nationalism' in the face of unwavering French repression. In 1975 the first confrontation occurred. An underground organisation was formed: the FLNC (Corsican National Liberation Front). Using heavily armed fighters, it tried to force the state to accept the idea of a genuine dialogue with regard to the island's interests.

In 1982, after hundreds of violent incidents had taken place, Corsica finally received a special statute and also an island parliament based in Ajaccio. However, the close-knit system of favouritism and nepotism that had established itself among all recognised parties during the decades of neglect now led to excessive land speculation for tourism projects, and the underground movement continued to resort to violence to express its disenchantment with developments.

Through the 1990s, bombings and assassinations intensified as the various factions and splinter groups of the FLNC began fighting each other for control of the organised crime networks that were funding their armed struggle. Successive administrations, meanwhile, tried to negotiate a political solution to the troubles, making little headway.

The situation came to a head in 1998, when the French Government's most senior representative on the island, Préfet Claude Erignac, was gunned down in Ajaccio. The outrage crystallised mounting opposition to separatist violence on the island, bringing the paramilitaries under pressure to come to the negotiating table.

The deadlock seemed finally to be giving way in 2003, when the Chirac government managed to push through a referendum on greater autonomy. But the package of proposals – featuring increased legislative and tax-raising powers for a new regional assembly, and increased status in schools for the Corsican language – was narrowly defeated at the polls. Since the setback, condemned by Paris as a 'wasted opportunity', nationalist violence has resurfaced, but it seldom, if ever, affects visitors. The only outward signs of the troubles are likely to be the Corsican names scrawled over French roadsigns and ubiquitous political graffiti. These days, most islanders recognise that without financial support from Paris, and revenue from tourism, Corsica would be an economic desert – an attitude which has thawed to a noticeable extent the Corsicans' famously frosty reaction to outsiders.

High season on the beach at Calvi

Historical Highlights

4,000BC The first *castelli* are built on the island.

1,500BC The Torréens subjugate Southern Corsica.

565BC Greeks from Asia Minor found the city of Alalia on the east coast.

259BC Roman conquests begin.

AD100 Christianity arrives on the island.

456 The Vandals destroy the coastal towns.

534 Byzantine Emperor Justinian I defeats the Vandals.

700 The Moors (Saracens) repeatedly terrorise the island – right into the 15th century.

774 Charlemagne presents Corsica to the Vatican.

1016 The Vatican entrusts Pisa with administration of the island.

1268 The Genoese found Calvi.

1284 Genoa defeats the Pisans.

1297 The Pope makes the King of Aragon new custodian of the island.

1380 The Genoese found Bastia.

1420 Bonifacio, founded in 828 by the Tuscan count of the same name, withstands the King of Aragon's siege.

1440 Genoa founds San Firenze (Saint-Florent).

1453 The city-republic of Genoa cedes administration of the island to the Bank of St George.

1492 Genoa has the citadel built in Ajaccio.

1553 Corsica is occupied by the French for the first time.

1559 The island is returned to Genoa under the terms of the Spanish-French peace treaty of Cateau-Cabresis.

1564 Sampiero, an officer of the Medicis and France, recaptures the island with his men. The Genoese have him killed in an ambush.

1725 Pasquale Paoli born in Merusaglia.

1729 The great revolt against the Genoese finally breaks out.

1731 Intervention of an Austrian army of mercenaries.

1735 A Corsican *consulta* calls for the establishment of an independent monarchy.

1736 Westphalian Baron von Neuhof is crowned King Theodore I.

1738 Second French intervention against Corsica.

1739 Corsica's political and military leaders go into exile.

1755 Pasquale Paoli is appointed national leader in the Castignaccia.

1768 Genoa sells off the island to France.

1769 Defeat of Corsican militia near Ponte Nuevo. Paoli exiled in England. Napoleon is born in Ajaccio.

1789 Corsica becomes a part of the French Empire.

1790 Paoli returns from exile.

1794–6 Corsica ruled by an English viceroy, Gilbert Elliot.

1807 Death of Pasquale Paoli.

1830 First steamship connection between Ajaccio and Bastia.

1914–18 During World War I, 30,000 Corsicans die for France.

1942 Corsica is occupied by fascist Italy.

1943 Corsica liberated by partisans and regular units.

1955–62 Around 17,500 French colonials from North Africa are presented with land on Corsica.

1975 Two *gendarmes* are killed during fighting with autonomists. The FNLC movement is formed.

1982 Corsica receives a special regional statute without any real rights.

1992 Statute extended with a regional executive. The nationalists receive one-quarter of the vote in the regional elections.

1998 Préfet Claude Erignac shot dead by nationalists in Ajaccio.

2003 Goatherd Yvan Colonna is arrested for Erignac's murder. Soon after, a referendum on a new package of devolutionary measures returns a 'No' vote from the islanders.

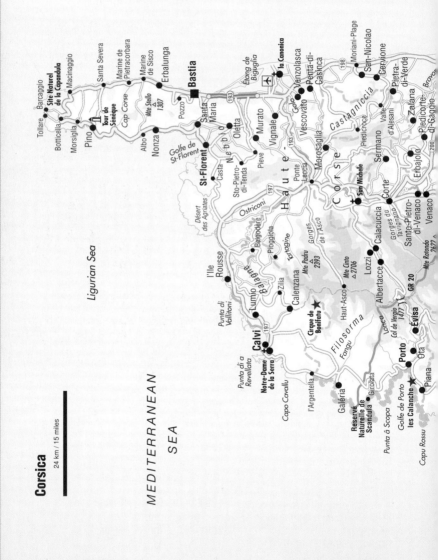

Corsica

24 km / 15 miles

MEDITERRANEAN SEA

Ligurian Sea

Tollare
Barcaggio
Site Naturel de la Capandula
Macinaggio
Santa Severa
Botticella
Morsiglia
Marine de Pietracorbara
Marine de Sisco
Pino
Tour de Sénèque
Erbalunga
Cap Corse
Mte Stello 1307
Bastia
Alba
Nonza
Pozzo
Santa Maria
Étang de Biguglia
la Canonica
Golfe de St-Florent
St-Florent
Casta
Nebbio
Oletta
Murato
Vignale
Vescovato
Venzolasca
Penta-di-Casinca
Moriani-Plage
San-Nicolao
Cervione
Pietra-di-Verde
Sto-Pietro-di-Tenda
Pieve
Ponte Leccia
Morosaglia
Piedicroce
Valle-d'Alesani
Zalana
Piedicroce-di-Verde
Bravona
Ostriconi
Désert des Agriates
Ponte Leccia
Castagniccia
Sermano
Erbajolo
Pledicorte-di-Gaggio
Belgodère
Pioggiola
Gorges de Tartagine
Gorges de l'Asco
Corte
Santo-Pietro-di-Venaco
l'Ile Rousse
Zilia
Calenzana
Mte Padru 2393
Mte Cinto 2706
Lozzi
Calacuccia
Gorges du Tavignano
San Michele
Venaco
Mte Rotondo 7677
Punta di Vallitoni
Tumlio Balagna
Albertacce
GR 20
Haut-Asco
Haute-Corse
Fangu
Cirque de Bonifatu
Calvi
Punta di a Revellata
Notre-Dame de la Serra
Filosorma
Golo
Lonca Col de Vergio 1477
Évisa
l'Argentella
Capo Cavallu
Galéria
Girolata
Ota
Porto
Punta à Scopa
Reserve Naturelle de Scandula
Golfe de Porto
les Calanche
Piana
Capu Rossu

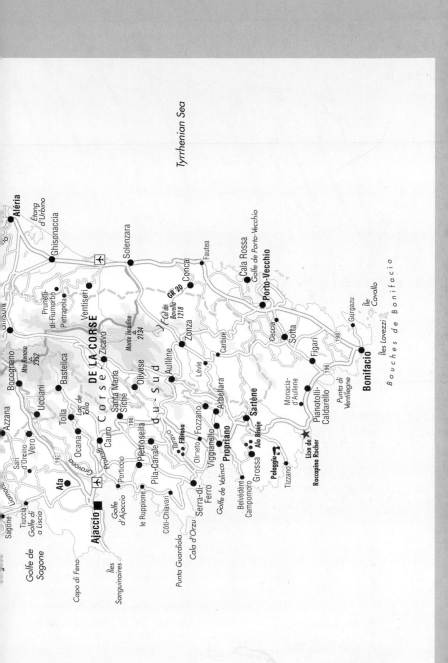

For an island as small as Corsica, the variety of landscape is really quite amazing. Behind the beaches there's a whole hinterland of adventure just waiting to be discovered. Even though I've lived here for so long, Corsica is still full of surprises for me, and I've shared many of them with you in this book in 14 day-trip suggestions based around the island's major centres.

Starting in Bastia, the most down-to-earth of Corsican towns with its distinctive Italian flair, the first trips take you round the **northeast** of the island, including a tour of its 'index finger', the Cap Corse with its quaint fishing settlements, the Patrimonio wine-growing district and the fabled Castagniccia region with its ancient hill villages – the very heartland of Corsican tradition.

Then we go up to the old country's secret capital of Corte from which you can explore some of the splendid scenery provided by the island's highest **mountains and towns**. The main road down the east coast brings you to Bonifacio, a town precariously perched on the clifftops and the departure point for a tour of the **south**, first to the medieval town of Sartène and then on to examine some much older vestiges of the island's long and eventful past. Ajaccio is the base for exploring the dramatic **west coast**, including the magnificent rock formations of the *calanches* and beautiful coastal villages such as Porto. Calvi in the **northwest** is dominated not only by its Genoese citadel, but also by the impressive hills of the Balagne rising in the background and studded with yet more picturesque villages. For all but the town tours I've assumed that you have your own private transport.

Take the ferry from France or Italy

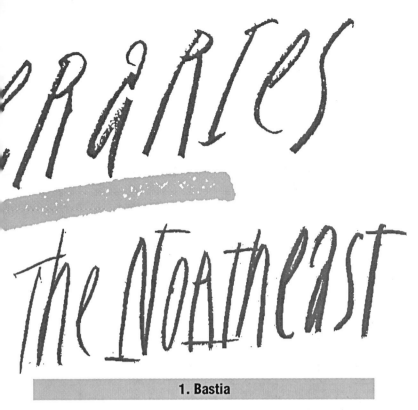

ITINERARIES

The Northeast

1. Bastia

Particularly for those who arrive by ferry, a tour of this Italian-flavoured town starting at Place Saint-Nicolas, and taking in shops, churches and markets in the Old Town, then the port, Citadel and church of Santa Maria. See map page 22.

Oddly enough, most people who have just been standing at a ferry's railing to watch this attractively situated town approaching tend to forgo its attractions altogether. Green road signs draw mo-

torists onward like a magnet, either up to Cap Corse or, directly at the harbour exit, straight down into a tunnel leading south-westwards: minutes later, Bastia is far behind.

But if travelling means absorbing the atmosphere of a foreign place, then Bastia is the perfect town in which to do it.

A few steps up from the ferry port you'll find yourself in the spacious **Place Saint-Nicolas** and in the thick of Corsican life: men playing *boules*, others talking or pacing up and down past the **statue of Napoleon** wrapped in a toga, and staring out to sea. Children with balls and tricycles next

Napoleon on the Place Saint-Nicolas

21

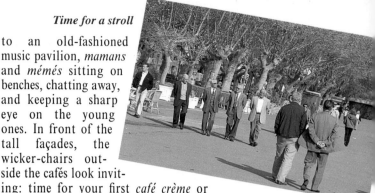

to an old-fashioned music pavilion, *mamans* and *mémés* sitting on benches, chatting away, and keeping a sharp eye on the young ones. In front of the tall façades, the wicker-chairs outside the cafés look inviting: time for your first *café crème* or *pastis*. Bastia is the most Italian of Corsica's towns. In clear weather the islands of Elba, Capraia and Monte Cristo are visible through the trees. In the pavilion housing the Office Municipal de Tourisme there is a hotel directory.

The line of cafés on the square continues on towards the south and down into the narrow **Rue Napoléon**, where it becomes a colourful mix of boutiques and bakeries, craft shops and tiny churches, among them the **Eglise Saint-Roch**, the result of a solemn promise made after a plague outbreak in 1598, and the far more magnificent **Chapelle de l'Immaculée Conception** (1704). In front of the latter's portal, colourful stones have been arranged to form a sun, and above the main altar you can admire a painting of the Murillo School.

Just behind this chapel a street leads off to the left, down to the morning market in the **Place de l'Hôtel de Ville**. All the smells and the colours of Corsica are here, and Mediterranean

[Map of Bastia]

Gare SNCF
Rond Point
Mal Leclerc
Palais de Justice
Bibliothèque Municipale
Cinéma le Regent
St-Charles
Rue Favalelli
Boulevard Paoli
Chemin de l'Hôpital Militaire
Théâtre
Av. Marechal Sebastiani
Blvd Auguste Gaudin
Opéra Municipal
Rue César Campinchi
(Rue de l'Opera)
Rue San Angelo
Cinéma Studio
Maison ou vécut H. de Balzac
Maison de l'Artisanat
Boulevard Paoli
(A Traversa)
Porto-Vecchio, Corte
R. César Vezzani
l'Immaculée Conception
Rue Napoleon
Rue du Colle
Blvd General de Gaulle
Av. Fr. Pietri
Pl. D. Vincetti
Pl. Prela
St-Jean Baptiste
Hôtel de Ville
St-Roch
Napoleon Monument
Place St-Nicolas
Mairie de Bast
Voie Rapide
Cours Dr. Favale
Pl. de l'Hôtel de Ville
LEP
Allee du 173e R.I.A.
Guichets SNCM
Porte Louis-XVI
Musée M d'Ethnographie Corse
Institute Regional d'Administration
Voie Rapide
Palais des Gouverneurs
Vieux Port
Rue des Zephirs
Ste-Marie
Q. de la Santé
Inscription Maritime
Gare Maritime
Oratoire Baroque Ste-Croix
Quartier des Pecheurs
Bassin St-Nicolas
La Citadelle
Jetée St Nicolas

Bastia
400 m / 440 yds

Piombino, Livorno   Gerona, Nice

22

fish glisten in the sunlight in front of the shops on the other side of the square. If you want to photograph anything here, though – even a pile of sausage slices – you need to ask for permission first. Perhaps they still believe in the *malocchju* (Evil Eye)? The first baguette you nibble at, or your first piece of *fiadone* should definitely be bought at **Jeanne Galli**, a short distance up the hill on the same side as the fishmongers. Almost all the houses in the Old Town are built above fine vaulted cellars like the ones here, and their beauty is only now being redis- covered.

The Vieux Port and Saint-Jean-Baptiste

Go straight back across the market, past the church of **Saint- Jean-Baptiste**, which has one of the most elaborate interiors in Corsica. Built in 1636, it was restored in the 18th century with an abundance (some say an over-abundance) of multicoloured marble. Some of Cardinal Fesch's Italian paint- ings decorate the walls, but they're not nearly as impressive as those in the Fesch Museum in Ajaccio *(see page 51)*. The church's im- mense twin campaniles loom dramatically above the Vieux Port, a view captured on nu- merous postcards.

It's only a few steps down to the **Vieux Port**. This is the seed from which the city originally sprang: a strip of sand between the cliffs where the fishermen used to leave their boats. To protect this landing-place the Genoese built a massive round tower on the rocks opposite in 1380. It was this *bastiglia* (now the Citadel) that gave the city its name – older Corsicans still pronounce it *Bashtia* with the stress on the second syllable. An elegant double flight of steps with a small stone land- ing lead up to the tower. It was later used to form a corner of the Governor's Palace, which today contains the **Musée d' Ethno- graphie** (currently closed for renovation work). Minerals, finds from antiquity, old etchings, a tattered flag dating from the last battle

Map labels:

The Northeast

8 km / 5 miles

- - - - Itinerary 2
- - - - Itinerary 3
- - - - Itinerary 4

Giraglia
Cap Corse
Capo Grosso Tollare Barcaggio
Site Naturel de la Capandula
Moulin Mattei Ersa
Centuri-Port Rogliano
Macinaggio
Morsiglia
Capo Corvoli Meria Marine de Meria
Couv. de St-Francois
Pino Luri 80
Barrettali Marine de Porticciolo
Monte Alticcione 1138 Pietracorbara Marine de Pietracorbara
Punta di Canelle Canari Tour de Castellare
Cannelle Cima di e Follice 1324 Sisco Marine de Sisco
Marine d'Albo Tour de Sacro
Tour Genoise Monte Stello 1307 Nonza Pozzo Erbalunga
Marine de Negru 80 Santa Maria di-Lota Lavasina
Marine de Farinole S. Martino di-Lota Miomo
Golfe de St-Florent Menhir Nativo Ste. Lucie
Santa Maria Patrimonio Bastia
St-Florent Barbaggio Citadelle
Sta-Maria Assunta Col de Teghime 536 **Ligurian Sea**
l'Aliso 81 193
Nebbio 82
Oletta
Sto-Pietro-di-Tenda Défilé de Lancone Casatorra
Gavino di Tenda 62 Borgo
Sorio Pieve San Michele Ile San Damianu
Murato Etang de Biguglia
Monte Tasso 1372 Cima di Taffoni 1117 Borgo
Campitello Scolca Lucciana La Cononica
Puerto Nuovo Plage de Pineto
193 Vescovato Casamozza
Corte Loreto-di-Casinca Fouilles de Mariana
Col Saint-Antoine Silvareccio Venzolasca
Giocatojo Penta-di-Casinca 198
71 237 Piano Folleli Alto
Morosaglia la Porta Talasani
Monte S. Petrone 1767 Campana Pietra Giusta 1183
San Quilico Piedicroce Moriani-Plage
Cambia Carcheto San-Nicolao
Rusio Carticasi Punta de Caldane 1724 Carpineto Faice
Col d'Arcarotta Cervione Prunete
Bustanico PARC NATUREL 71 198
Sermano RÉGIONAL DE LA CORSE
San Nicolao Mazzola Pietra-di-Verde Chiatra Aléria

---

against the French... You're sure to understand the island better after a visit here.

The view from the parapet of the Citadelle stretches right across the city and its three harbours. The Rue Sainte-Croix leads up to the side facade of the church of **Ste Maria**, and access to the adjoining Holy Ghost Chapel at the back is through a gateway on the left. The Holy Cross *(Sainte Croix)*, with its figure of Christ carved in ebony, is meant to possess miraculous powers, and according to legend was found floating in the sea by some fishermen in 1428. The church proper, located just around the corner, contains a silver Madonna, Italian paintings and an organ from the Serassi brothers' workshop in Bergamo.

Though strongly influenced by northern Italy, Bastia is also an accurate reflection of the French lifestyle. The noisy city traffic thunders down the Boulevard Paoli, in which the latest Paris fashions and perfumes contrast sharply with the old narrow alleyways just a few steps away, festooned with washing-lines and so reminiscent of the back streets of Naples.

Most of the city's bistros and restaurants are clustered in the streets around the Vieux Port, **A Casarelle** and **u Tiaus** being two particularly good choices. **La Citadelle**, situated above the port, only a few steps away from the *bastiglia*, is inexpensive at lunchtime and becomes a real gourmet haven in the evenings.

2. Cap Corse

A trip around the Cap Corse is just 123km/76 miles long (starting and finishing in Bastia), but it takes a whole day. Magnificent views, watch-towers, a black beach and the finest harbour on the island are just a few of the attractions along the way. See map opposite.

To avoid being blinded by the morning and afternoon sun, I strongly recommend that you do the trip around the Cap Corse in a clockwise direction, starting on the west coast. To get there from Bastia, pick up the signs to Saint-Florent at the roundabout in front of the ferry terminal. The D81 snakes up past the Monastery of Saint-Antoine, and reaches the top of the **Col de Teghime** (536m/1,760ft), which provides stunning views of both coasts. The pass is marked by a German army anti-tank gun.

The road winds its way down towards the west coast of Cap Corse through the little villages that form part of the **Patrimonio** wine-growing region (*see page 29*). Just after the village of Patrimonio, take the D80, which you'll be following for the rest of the day, off to the right. It meets the coast at **Marine de Farinole**, and a short distance to the north the hairpin bend at **Marina di Negru** provides another magnificent view, this time southwards across the Golfe de Saint-Florent and all the way to Monte Cinto.

Nonza appears just after you've passed a mausoleum. Its houses lie huddled against the slope. Above them you can see the square Genoese tower − once the scene of a heroic achievement: in 1768, a disabled lieutenant called **Casella** held this tower against a force of 1,200 French troops, using his courage and wit. His fellow-soldiers had deserted him, so he placed their guns in the gaps along the battlements and fired them one after the other, shouting commands all the while. Once all his powder was used up, he came out on crutches − alone.

An unexpected sight awaits you at the other end of the village. Lean out over the parapet next to the church; below, you will see 3km (2 miles) of greyish-black beach (a hazardous side-effect of asbestos mining), turning even the sea beyond the white line of foam a strange colour − a mixture of turquoise and violet. Tourists like to spell their names on the beach here using light-coloured pebbles. A path leads down through some overgrown gardens, and

The view from Nonza

past a double fountain called the **Fontaine Sainte-Julie**. St Julie wasn't martyred here in Nonza, but in Carthage in the year 303, where she had both her breasts cut off.

To reach the tower you have to cross the small square opposite the church. To the south there is a fine view of the pastel-coloured mosaic formed by the various slate roofs, and also northwards straight down to the beach, through a well-placed hole in the rock.

At its very end, in **Albo**, the road around the Cap goes right past the colourful pebbles and a fine tower. Swimming here when the waves are high is quite dangerous because of the strong undertow. The small Hotel Morganti retains its old-fashioned charm, in the face of the more modern buildings around it.

Exchanging pleasantries in Nonza

From here there are two worthy digressions from the D80. To the north, the scars left on the hillside by the abandoned asbestos mine are not pretty. If you take the road up towards Pieve, a hamlet in the village of **Canari**, however, the white bell-tower with its clock, 300m (1,000ft) above the sea, looks striking. Further up stands a wonderfully well-preserved Pisan chapel, **Santa Maria Assunta**, dating from the 12th century and decorated with enigmatic stone carvings. From behind it, you can follow a signposted footpath into the *maquis* and up towards the summit of Cap Corse's highest peak, **Cime a e Folicce** (1,324m/4,344ft), reachable after 3–4 hours of stiff climbing. It's among the island's most memorable walks, but you'll need a decent map, good footwear and an early start to reach the top before the clouds bubble up around 11am. Downhill, the D33 travels past the baroque church of **Saint-François**. A gravestone in front of the altar shows the touching figure of Vittoria de Gentile holding her swaddled child.

Barrettali is also high up, and near Mineviu there are some magnificent mausoleums next to the road. From **Morsiglia**, take the D35 down to **Centuri Port**, which may be the most picturesque harbour on the island: blue-and-white fishing boats, nets, rigging of all colours and terraces all around on which the day's catch gets placed. The speciality along this rocky coastline is crayfish *(langouste)*. With the sights and the food here, hours pass by in a flash. You're not pressed for time, though: it's only 58km (36 miles) around the Cap to Bastia.

The round towers in the area once had windmill-sails. Today a modern wind farm carries on the tradition. This village is where we say farewell to the western side of the Cap Corse. If you turn around you'll find yourself looking at the island of **Giraglia** with its massive **lighthouse**. From Ersa, two roads lead to Tollare and Barcaggio on a

Erbalunga

round trip covering 16km (10 miles). From the 12th to the 16th century the Da Mare family, the Tuscan rulers of this area, used to live in **Rogliano**. Their ruined castles, churches and ornate tombs all testify to the incredible power they once wielded. In **Macinaggio**, Paoli's former naval base, Italian yachts can be seen jostling one another in the harbour. The town marks the start of a great coastal walk, the **Sentier du Douanier**, which heads north through the idyllic Site Naturel de la Capandula and skirts the tip of Cap Corse to reach Barcaggio in three hours. The local tourist office hands out free maps, but you can easily follow the route without one as it's unobstructed and signposted.

From here the road is wider and driving easier. You pass a few beaches, the surprisingly well-preserved **Tour de Losse**, and **Erbalunga** – with its ultra-narrow streets, intimate piazzas and tower. The restaurant with its balcony above the harbour is called, naturally enough, **Le Pirate**. **Lavasina** is a place of pilgrimage; the 16th-century Madonna above the marble altar has been ascribed to the **Perugino** school. The church also stands at the head of the 5-hour trail up **Monte Stello**, Cap Corse's second-highest peak, from where a superb panorama extends over the north of the island and across to the Italian coast. The route is well marked with blue paint. With a car you could drive the first stretch as far as the hamlet of **Pozzo**, just above Erbalunga, saving yourself a couple of hours' uphill walk through thick *maquis*.

3. The Conca d'Oru

From Bastia to Conca d'Oru, the 'Golden Conch' and bread-basket of Corsica above the Golfe de Saint-Florent. See map on page 24.

Follow the N193 out of Bastia in the direction of Ajaccio and Calvi. Around 9km (5½ miles) further along this motorway, a sign points off to Col de Stefano (D62) to the right, into the **Défilé de Lancone**, a ravine created by the inconspicuous little Bevinco River. The short winding route emerges at the **Col de San Stefano**, and one of the five routes that meet up here, the D5, leads off to the left, to **Murato**. Just a few minutes later, on a meadowy slope, stands the Pisan-Romanesque church of **San Michele**, undisputedly the finest church on Corsica. Its anonymous builders used a combination of serpenine from the Bevinco valley and white, yellow and even reddish marble to create a superb harmony that seems almost accidental. This church, 20 paces long and eight paces wide, has some magnificent ornaments, symbols and naive

The church of San Michele

Fish are landed at Saint-Florent

figures on its facade, and below the slate roof of the apse there is also another relief frieze visible, dating from an earlier chapel. The belltower, placed on pillars in front of the portal, is unique on the island. The interior contains frescoes as well as carved reliefs from the previous structure on the site, dating from the 10th century. The church remains open in daylight hours; if it's closed, ask for the keys at the *mairie* in Murato (open Mon–Sat 9am–noon and 2–5pm).

A very different artistic experience awaits you in the former **monastery church** in the village. Behind the portal on the right, the *condottiere* Romano Murato had himself included in a picture of Mary Magdalene which he commissioned from Titian or one of his pupils. If the church is closed, just ask at the *mairie (see above)*.

After this you can either drive through a handful of sleepy villages under cliff-faces around the fertile valley basin of the **Conca d'Oru** and take the extremely sinuous D62 towards the sea, or you can head back towards Saint-Florent along a somewhat faster route. For the latter, drive back to the Col San Stefano and from there to **Oletta**. This village, which was once the capital of Corsica's former wheat-growing region, still has the reputation of baking excellent bread. The D82 leads straight to the **Golfe de Saint-Florent** from here. Roughly halfway along the route you should turn off left and take a look at the **Poterie d'Oletta**, with its superb traditional ceramics.

You should reach Saint-Florent just before noon. There's a large car park on the left when you reach the harbour. If you take a stroll through the narrow streets to the right of the Hôtel de l'Europe and to the square where they play *boules*, you'll come across a shop selling jewellery made of Corsican coral. There are pleasant restaurants next to the water's edge. The little sandy beach opposite – Plage de la Roya – can be reached from the end of the Oletta road

The limestone Menhir Nativo

by turning sharp right after the bridge or on foot via the pedestrian bridge in the marina.

On the right, behind the Bar du Passage at the flower-bed with the war memorial, a narrow street leads to the nearby **Santa Maria Assunta** (open July and Aug 5–8pm; key from tourist office, but you'll need some form of ID as security), the Pisan cathedral of the Nebbio. Nebbio (Nebbiu) means fog (after the mists that linger over the basin in spring and autumn), and the town that once bore the name, infested with malaria and destroyed by the Moors, was eventually abandoned completely in the 13th century. A glass shrine inside the church contains the mummified remains of the martyr and patron saint **Saint Flor**, presented to the church by the Vatican in 1771. The key to the church can be obtained from the Office de Tourisme in the modern administration building on the left as you leave the town towards Bastia.

Bastia is actually only 23km (14 miles) away, via the **Col de Teghime**, so you can take your time in the wine-growing area of **Patrimonio**. Almost all the growers here will invite you to a free *dégustation* so that you can test their reds, whites and rosés. In the village, to the left of the impressive church, a sign points the way to the **Menhir Nativo**. This is the only known menhir statue on the island that is made of limestone, and it was discovered in 1964 when a vineyard was being ploughed in a hamlet called Barbaggio further up the hill. The roughly 3,000-year-old sculpture now stands to the left of the village war memorial, under a little roof to protect it from the weather.

4. The Castagniccia

The mountains of the Castagniccia dominate the northeastern plain. The region gets its name from the ancient chestnut trees that grow here. Lunch in La Porta, with the possibility of a swim at Moriani-Plage before returning to Bastia. See map on page 24.

La Canonica

Passing beneath the Vieux Port, follow the N193 out of Bastia heading south, past the town's ugly industrial suburbs. After about 17km (10½ miles), turn off to the left in the direction of Poretta Airport, and then right again almost immediately, following signs to the Hotel La Madrague. The D10 passes the hotel and then leads straight to the 12th-century Pisan church of Santa Maria Assunta, known as a **Canonica** because the bishops and their canons once used to reside in an adjoining building. It is the oldest surviving basilica on the island, whose only decoration is the geometric pattern carved into the southern facade. A few of the foundation walls and a beautiful mosaic floor nearby attest to the existence of a Roman settlement – the legionaries' colony called **Mariana**. An Early Christian basilica and a 4th-century baptistry used to stand here before they were destroyed by the Lombards. After that the Mariana was threatened in turn by the Vandals, the Moors and by malaria – and it was finally abandoned in the 9th century.

Back again now to the N193, which continues on in the direction of Bonifacio and now becomes the N198. The second road to the right after the bridge over the Golo leads up to **Vescovato** in the Casinca. Just minutes away from the main coast road on the D6, this place is another world entirely. In a small square surrounded by plane trees, four ugly gargoyles spew out mountain water into a cast-iron fountain. Houses tower above, and here and there the odd trace of coloured plaster stands as a reminder of the time when this place took over the role of bishopric after Mariana had been abandoned–a secure refuge high above the perpetually threatened plain.

After Venzolasca, turn right on the D6 towards **Loreto-di-Casinca**. This village, with its prominent campanile, seems close enough to touch, but keeps disappearing behind bends in the road. Soon Venzolasca lies far below, like a toy village, with the Etang de Biguglia spread out behind it. The predominantly elderly population of Loreto goes about its business: in the narrow road leading up to the campanile, doors stand wide open – little grocery shops that don't need name-boards because everyone knows everyone else.

Turn right along the D237 through the tiny villages of **Silvareccio** and **Piano** and towards the **Col Saint-Antoine**. You will notice that some of the slopes have chestnut trees on them. Formerly, chestnuts were used by the islanders to feed their animals, they were exchanged for oil and wine, they were *glacé* as *marrons de Nice*, and they were ground to make flour, or baked. Up on the pass (688m/2,250ft) behind the ivy and cypress trees on the right stands the tower of the ruined monastery of **Saint-Antoine**. It was within these walls in 1755 that Pasquale Paoli was appointed chief of the Corsican nation by a *consulta* shortly after his return from exile. Before you get to the fork in the pass, turn sharp left and carry on along the D515 to – according to the map – **Giocatojo**, which, however, now announces itself proudly as Ghjucatoghju. It lies on the edge of the **Parc Régional Naturel**, which was extended in 1992. The village is on

Fountain in Loreto-di-Casinca

Village balcony

a narrow ridge, with its church at the top. The road drops down through shady sections of forest alternating with sun-scorched clearings to reach the church square of **La Porta**.

The clumsy restoration of the free-standing campanile next to the baroque church incurred the wrath of many a Corsican. But you can stop here for lunch, at the unpretentious restaurant **Chez Elisabeth** (tel: 04 95 39 22 00) on the left of the iron fountain, which has a terrace jutting out over the valley below.

Hoar-frost, sometimes as late as Easter, and chestnut leaves and moss in autumn can make the roads around here slippery and treacherous. So even if you've calmly taken your time while sampling Corsican dishes in Chez Elisabeth or in Piedicroce (**Le Refuge**), don't suddenly feel you need to hurry. Just before you reach Piedicroce on the D71 you can see the tiny village of **Campana**, with its chapel above the road. The large painting behind the altar, an **Adoration of the Shepherds**, is a masterpiece of the Seville school and probably by Francisco Zurbarán (1598–1664). Ask for the key at the *mairie* opposite. Shortly after this on the left you can see the fenced-in ruins of the **Couvent d'Orezza**, a symbol of Corsican rejection of Genoese rule. It was here in 1731 that the islanders asked themselves whether a rebellion was in keeping with Christian teachings. Ten years later, in the same place, part of Paoli's constitution was passed. During the last battles on the island in 1944 the building, reduced to the role of an ammunition depot, was blown to pieces.

Down in the valley lies **Orezza**, once a spa resort with its own spring, now revived as a production centre of bubbly mineral water. At the entrance to the village of **Carcheto**, brown-coloured 'Parc Régional Naturel' signs point the way down to a waterfall and to the church of **Santa Mar-**

Man and herd

garita. It's worth asking for the key here, too. The 15 naive pictures of the Stations of the Cross in the nave were painted by an unknown Castagniccia artist, who used foresters as models.

Continuing along the D71, you'll reach the highest point of this round trip at the **Col d'Arcarotta** (819m/2,700ft). Several villages can be seen far below on both sides; in the summertime the local craftsmen and smallholders hold a Sunday market up here. Over to the right, the huge **Punta de Caldane** (1,724m/5,650ft) blocks the way to the **Bozio** (*see page 38*). From this point it's downhill through the numerous hamlets of Felce. Further towards the sea, the landscape gets increasingly bare and desolate. Chiatra can be seen silhouetted against the reservoir at **Alesani**; its water is used to irrigate crops on the island's eastern plain.

The road now splits up again, with the left fork going off towards **Cervione**. This town was briefly the residence of King Theodore; now even the finest of its buildings are falling to pieces, although the cathedral of Bishop Alexander, formerly known to the Corsicans as *Lisandru*, has been well restored. Just past it on the left the **Museu Etnugraficu** (open daily except Sun and public holidays, 9am–noon and 2.30–6pm; admission charge) will give you a good general impression of the history of the Castagniccia.

Where geraniums flourish

Another short detour before the coast leads along a narrow, seldom-used road that has been blasted out of the rock, in the direction of **San Nicolao**. From the stopping-places along here there are some excellent views to be had of the vineyards and citrus plantations on the flood-plain below. You pass a waterfall between two tunnels, and then the road winds its way on down to **Moriani-Plage**. The sea is straight ahead, and you're on the 100-km (60-mile) long beach that stretches from Bastia to Solenzara. On the right-hand side of the passageway leading to the promenade, on the wall of an old fisherman's hut, you'll see a plaque: Ghjacinto Paoli sailed into exile in Italy from here, and in 1755 his son Pasquale came ashore to save the nation.

Bastia is an hour's drive northwards along the coast road.

5. Corte and the Niolo

Through the Scala di Santa Regina and into the Niolo. A tour of the island's finest forests at the foot of Monte Cinto (2,706m/8,891ft). Then an afternoon stroll through Corte. See map on page 35.

Corte, the Corsicans' secret capital, is the perfect base for excursions into superb mountain scenery. You can stay in town or try the **Hotel Colonna** at the entrance to the **Restonica Valley**.

After breakfast, drive north along Cours Paoli away from Place Paoli. After the bridge over the River Orta, take the D18 that branches off sharp left in a northerly direction. After around 20 minutes you'll reach **Pont de Castirla**. If you want to eat here later today it's best to reserve a table now in the restaurant on the right called **Chez Jacqueline** (tel: 04 95 47 42 04).

The **Scala di Santa Regina** begins on the other side of the Golo bridge, on the left. It is rough, full of bends, and at its upper end it used to be almost impossible to get through, until this road was completed in 1989. The ravine's name means 'staircase of the holy queen' and comes from the mule-path which used to wind its way over this threshold of reddish, almost bare granite in huge bends. The River Golo descends 550m (1,800ft) between one end of the ravine and the other.

The valley suddenly broadens out, and you'll see the reservoir at the foot of the highest mountain on the island, **Monte Cinto** (2,706m/8,900ft). To the right, above Calacuccia, several villages

Mist hangs in the Scala de Santa Regina

are clustered across its southern slope, including the remote **Calasima** (1,095m/3,600ft), Corsica's highest village, above which the amazingly steep and jagged **Paglia Orba** (2,525m/8,300ft) dominates the view.

Even a valley basin as remote as this one was populated as long ago as the Stone Age. Beyond Calacuccia, between L'Acqua Viva hotel-cum-filling station and Le Corsica restaurant, you can see a **dolmen** over to the left on a meadowy rise. The road now leads up towards the watershed to the southwest, passing through some of the finest forests on the island. The Laricio pine trees here are 40m (130ft) or more in height. Some of the larger ones are over 600 years old, and measure up to 2m (6½ft) at the base. Their high tops create a lot of shade – hence the name **Valdo Niello**, or 'Black Forest'.

The highest section of road on the island is the **Col de Vergio** (1,477m/4,850ft), marked by an enormous and very modern statue of the Virgin; the view from up here extends back across the Calacuccia Reservoir. On the other side of the pass the road then descends in a series of steep curves to Porto, on the west coast (*see page 55*).

Alternatively, you could stretch your legs here with a pleasant walk up the **Golo Valley**. A well-signposted trail winds north from the car park through the pine forest, emerging after an hour or so at the Golo River, which crashes through a spectacular sequence of waterfalls and deep pools that are ideal for bathing. In the background, the south face of mighty Paglia Orba rises from the head of the valley, making this one of the most dramatic corners of the island.

This area's other popular day walk is up to **Lac de Nino** (1,762m/ 5,780ft), beginning at a bend in the Col de Vergio–Calacuccia road (D84) known as the 'Fer de Cheval', or 'Horseshoe'. Indicated by yellow markers, the path takes three hours of strenuous walking to complete, but the effort is amply rewarded. The lake is framed by snow-streaked mountains, with grassy shores grazed by herds of wild pigs and horses. Determined walkers can continue along the Tavignano River, which rises at the lake, as far as the Refuge A Sega (another three hours), from where a classic walk takes you down the Tavignano Gorge to Corte in around four hours.

Otherwise, at the end of the forest, just after the bridge over the River Golo, a road on the right leads to **Casamaccioli**. This sleepy village wakes up on 8 September each year when the **A**

The defiant General Gaffori, Corte

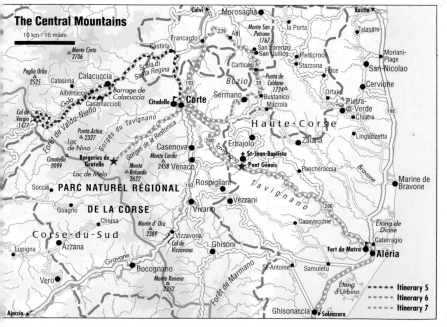

Wild horses above Casamaccioli

Santa di Niolo is celebrated – the Festival of the Virgin. A procession follows a statue of the Virgin and Child rescued from a monastery destroyed by the Turks in 1450. The monks, it is said, decided to let the statue choose its new sanctuary, and loaded it on to the back of a mule. Though the mule was not from the Niolo, he apparently trotted straight to Casamaccioli and stopped where the church is today.

On the southern side of the lake, past the dam, your journey takes you back through the Scala di Santa Regina again. You can stop for lunch at Chez Jacqueline. Remember, though, that you'll only make it back here by midday if you set off early enough and avoid the attractions of a walk in the forest along the way.

There is free parking in **Corte** below the Cours Paoli off the side-road leading to the university. At the end of the Cours, you can see the large bronze statue of the famous freedom-fighter **Paoli** – paid for by 'grateful Corsica' in 1864. Behind it a steep flight of wide, flat steps leads up to a statue of **General Gaffori** standing with his back to his house; its facade still bears traces of the Genoese siege.

A relief on the plinth of the statue relates the story of his courageous wife, Faustina. In 1746, her husband's men stormed the Citadel containing the Genoese who had managed to kidnap General Gaffori's young son. As they held him up to view on the battlements in order to obtain free passage, Faustina encouraged her compatriots to shoot all the same – the little boy remained unharmed. Four years later, the Genoese took advantage of Gaffori's absence to storm his home.

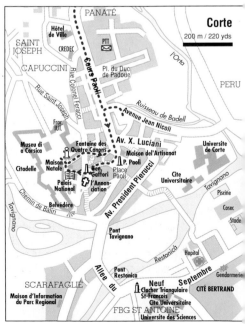

Village people

The Corsican soldiers defending it were on the point of surrendering to the Genoese when Faustina, clutching a blunderbuss, walked over to some barrels of gunpowder and pointed it at them, saying she'd blow up the house with everyone in it rather than surrender. She thus gained valuable time before reinforcements arrived.

Gaffori's outstretched arm points to the left towards the artisans' quarter and the **Belvédère**, a small platform with a view down to the city and up to the Citadel. To reach the main gate of the latter, climb up some more steps on the right-hand side of the Place Gaffori.

Here, you'll pass the birthplace of Napoleon's brother Joseph, who later became King of Spain and Naples, and then the **Palais National** (Palazzu Naziunale), seat of the government of Corsica from 1755 to 1769. The Citadel is undergoing a new lease of life: there is an **information office** just past the main gate; in the same building, the Parc Naturel provides details of its hiking routes *(randonnées pédestres)*; art exhibitions are held here; and the Citadel also contains various institutes forming part of the University of Corsica, situated just below the town. Though founded in 1765 by Paoli, the university was only re-opened in 1982. The central portion of the Citadel now accommodates the island's state-of-the-art **Museu di a Corsica** (open daily 10am–8pm; admission charge), where you can browse a huge collection of 3,000 or more artefacts amassed by a Catholic priest, Révérand Louis Doazan, in the 1950s. Temporary exhibitions also showcase aspects of contemporary island life.

At the northern end of the square in front of the Citadel, steps lead down to the **Fontaine des Quatre Canons** and then on to the Cours Paoli. **U Museu**, huddled at the foot of the Citadel walls on the cobbled Rampe Ribanelle, offers various good-value menus of Corsican specialities: get there early enough and you can sit at one of the tables outside looking across the rooftops of the Old Town to the valley.

6. Two Mountain Worlds

By car through the Gorges de la Restonica and a morning hike up to the Melo mountain lake (1,711m/5,600ft). Then, a round trip through the villages of the Bozio. See map on page 35.

Follow the signs to the **Gorges de la Restonica** along the D623 from Corte. The road starts off smooth, but soon a series of hairpins takes you higher above the mountain river, across stone bridges devoid of any parapet.

The Gorges de la Restonica

In contrast to the almost completely bare Scala di Santa Regina, this ravine has chestnut trees and Laricio pine dotted across its ochre-coloured rocky walls. About two-thirds of the way along, the road switches over to the right bank, and soon the trees are far behind. The car park at the **Bergeries de Grotelle** (1,375m/ 4,500ft), a group of shepherds' huts, is 45 minutes' drive away.

From the car park, the route continues on foot. Strong boots and a dependable waterproof coat are required if you plan to attempt the hour-long ascent to the first of the two high lakes cradled by this vertiginous landscape, **Lac de Melo**. Another 40 minutes' steep climb brings you to the picturesque and serene **Lac de Capitello**, hemmed in by sheer walls of boulders, from where there is an uninterrupted view of Monte Rotondo (2,622m/8,602ft), Corsica's second-highest peak.

It's possible to press on even further uphill from here to the ridge marking the island's watershed, traversed by the red-and-white waymarks of the GR20. Turn left (southeast) when you reach the path junction. After a convoluted 45-minute scramble through giant granite pinnacles and outcrops, keep your eyes peeled for a yellow-waymarked trail dropping steeply back downhill to Lac de Melo, where you can pick up the path to the car park. Back at the Bergeries de Grotelle, you can reward yourself with a giant sandwich from the shepherds' hut, filled with smoked meat and pungent local ewe's cheese.

This spectacular round route should take around four hours in dry conditions; given the altitude and exposed nature of some stretches, adequate clothing, water, a map and map-reading skills are essential, and be sure to check the weather forecast before you leave.

A room with a view

Another wonderful walk in the Restonica Valley is the ascent of **Monte Rotondo** (2,622m/8,602ft), which begins 11km (7 miles) from Corte, before the road crosses the river (look for a red spray-painted sign on your left). Red and yellow waymarks guide you up a relentlessly tough route comprising 3,360m (11,024ft) of ascent and descent. Most walkers only get far as the beautiful **Lac d'Oriente**, a secluded high-altitude lake reached after around 2½ hours. From here on, the terrain gets rockier as you traverse a huge moraine and scale a narrow chimney to reach the summit ridge; the trek then involves some exposed scrambling. Allow 8–9 hours for the whole climb and descent, not including rest breaks. It's worth noting that some of the higher sections may be badly iced up until the end of June, and the top of the mountain frequently gets a covering of cloud by midday. Again, check the weather forecast before setting off; and take adequate food, clothing and water.

The **Relais du Lac**, along the road on the other side of the bridge, serves delicious trout straight from the mountain stream.

After lunch make an afternoon visit to the area northeast of Corte known as the **Bozio** (U Boziu). This is the back door of the Castagniccia *(see page 29)*, and rarely visited by tourists. From Corte, take the N193 in the direction of Bastia. Past **Francardo**, take the D239 to **Aiti**; it heads back through town before it branches off between a chapel and Rex Bar; a less narrow and more comfortable alternative would be to travel 4km (2 miles) or so further on, and take the D39 over a bridge across the River Golo. The drive up to Aiti, though, with its seemingly endless hairpin bends, has a treat in store: opposite the tiny village, on the other side of the valley, you will gain a superb view of **Monte San Petrone** (1,767m/5,800ft) and of the rough mountain ridge in front of the Castagniccia.

Now take the road that descends steeply. On the other side of the bridge across the Casaluna, turn sharp right onto the D39, in the direction of Cambia and Carticasi. Beyond San Lorenzo,

The church in Sermano

just before a turn off to Carsoli, a dirt track, passable by four-wheel-drive vehicles only leads up to the Chapelle Santa Maria Menhir hermitage. If you carry on via the D99 a smoother road leads to **San Quilico** (about 2km/1 mile) with its Romanesque chapel containing 16th-century frescoes. The road comes to an end in this tiny hamlet; nevertheless, the short descent is worth it for a chance to see the wall paintings here. The little chapel's front and side entrances have symbolic figures carved into the stone. Eve can be seen taking the apple of temptation from the serpent's mouth, and there is also a figure wearing a belt – St Michael, perhaps – clutching a dragon-like serpent with his left hand and drawing a short sword with his right. The odd thing about this remote building is that it wasn't constructed until 1576; Pisan architectural style seems to have lasted longer in this remote area.

Beyond the pass above **Bustanico**, the Bozio suddenly opens up to the south, soaking up the warmth of the sun even in the cooler months of the year. The view stretches far across the Tavignano basin to the **Monte d'Oro** and **Monte Rotondo** near the Lac de Melo. The uprising against the Genoese broke out in Bustanico in 1729, when a tax-collector deprived an old man of his very last penny, and finally ended four decades later when the island was subjugated by the French. Bustanico's parish church, just below the main road through the village, contains an impressive 18th-century crucifix. The next village, **Sermano**, has, along with the village of Rusio, kept up the ancient tradition of the *paghjella* in its religious festivals *(see pages 79–81)*. Thanks to these two villages, this polyphonic form of singing has been given a new lease of life. As you descend towards the Tavignano in the late afternoon, you can see **Castellare-di-Mercurio**, on its narrow outcrop, silhouetted against the mountain scenery. Back down in the valley once more, turn right. Corte is just 6km (4 miles) away.

7. Corte to Bonifacio

From Corte, through the Tavignano Valley, to the ancient ruins of Aléria. Along the east coast to the primeval fortress of Arraggiu (Arraghju) near Porto-Vecchio, and then past some fine beaches to Bonifacio. See maps on pages 35 and 45.

This route has several longish stretches, but also fewer stops. It takes you from the northern to the southern half of the island. In Corte, follow the white arrow to **Aléria** before you reach the railway station,

The Genoese bridge

and after the roundabout go under a bridge and join the N200 which follows the Tavignano down towards the east coast. After a quarter of an hour, the road swings across a Genoese-built bridge to the north bank of the river. The bridge is very solidly built: its three stone arches have not only withstood the mountain torrents for centuries, but have also survived the strains of motor traffic. On the other side is the equally solidly built **Chapel of Saint-Jean-Baptiste**, dating from the 10th century. It was used as a refuge by shepherds for generations, and contains several ornamental inscriptions.

The foothills of the Castagniccia now force the Tavignano, and with it the road as well, down into a winding ravine, before the valley opens up to reveal the coast. In **Cateraggio** turn right on to the N198, and from the bridge over the Tavignano, the little village of Aléria can already be seen on the higher bank opposite. Towering above it is the **Fort de Matra**, which today houses the **Musée Jérôme Carcopino** (open daily 8am–noon and 2–7pm; admission charge), containing all the archaeological finds from excavations on the flood-plain. There are relics dating from the Stone, Bronze and Ice Ages, and some fine Greek vases that were found in the necropolis at the foot of the plateau, showing Bacchic and erotic scenes. The Carthaginians left blown glass behind, the Etruscans left drinking-horns or 'rhytons' shaped like dogs' and mules' heads, and the Roman exhibits are mostly practical: coins, oil-lamps and amphorae. The remains of the **Roman city of Aléria**, which in its heyday had a population of 20,000, are situated on a plateau southwest of the village.

Near the mouth of the Tavignano, the **Etang de Diane** forms a natural harbour which the Romans used as their naval base. From here, grain, olive oil, honey, wine, cork-bark, fish and mussels from the lagoon were shipped to Rome, just a day away by boat. Oysters were also transported, salted, in amphorae. Today, sea bass *(loup)* and kingfish are also bred here as well as in the **Etang**

The excavations at Aléria

d'Urbino further to the south. On both lagoons you can have your food fished out for you, at restaurants situated at the water's edge.

It takes another half hour to get to **Solenzara** (Sulinzara). If you feel the urge to get back into the mountains at this point, you can take an 80-km (50-mile) trip up to the **Col de Bavella** (1,218m/3,990ft) with its crenellated ridges, reminiscent of the Dolomites. You'll be getting almost a finer view of it though – from a bit further away and from its other side – if you follow *Itinerary 9 (see page 44)*.

The afternoon today can thus be spent in a more relaxing and equally interesting manner down near the coast.

Around 30km (12 miles) beyond Solenzara, the D559, closely followed by the D759, branches off in the direction of **Arraghju**. Brown 'Parc Naturel' signs lead you to a house with a car park on its left, and a sign to **Castellu** on its right. Walk across the courtyard, then cross some stepping-stones over a stream, and after a very steep 20-minute climb you'll finally reach a fortress made of reddish stone, situated imposingly on a small rise. It is one of the largest and most intact Torréen

Take a break

fortresses, whose structure even contains a basin for collecting rainwater, built into the rock. The view from here extends from the **Golfe de Pinarellu** as far as the **Golfe de Porto-Vecchio**.

As you enter **Porto-Vecchio** (Porti-Vecchju), follow the signs to the harbour *(Port)* at the roundabout just outside the town. If traffic isn't too bad you could drive directly to the centre, and through the **Porte Genoise**. There are parking spaces at the Hôtel de Ville or further down on either side of the main exit to Bastia. The **Place de L'Eglise**, surrounded by cafés, is very charming, and from the Porte Genoise there is a view of the salt pans on the other side of the harbour. Otherwise the town doesn't have any memorable sights.

Shortly after the exit in the direction of Bonifacio a sign on the left points the way towards **Palombaggia**. Its beaches, framed by red cliffs and broad, shady umbrella pines, lie at the end of a small side-road opposite the **Iles Cerbicale**. Out of season, this place is a dream. However, the collection of villas, bungalow villages and apartments on the slopes gives you a good idea of the sheer crush it can become at some times of the year.

Bonifacio, the destination for today, is just half an hour away, along the *route nationale*. There are three hotels in the Old Town, equipped with every modern convenience: **Le Genovese** up on the corner of the inlet, the three-star **Le Roy d'Aragon** down at the quayside and between them, halfway up the upper part of the town, **Le Royal**. The latter is very good value.

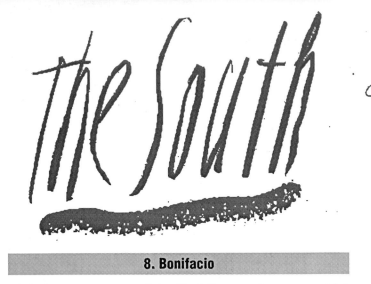

8. Bonifacio

Walk the narrow streets of the Citadelle up to the cemetery high above the ocean then sail along the coastline. See map opposite.

Perched atop cliffs, the upper part of the town naturally has no need of a defensive wall on its seaward side. On the other side the broad Montée Rastello, with its flat steps, leads up to the imposing city walls. Drive past the **Oratoire Saint-Roch**. Sixty metres (200ft) below, the sea crashes onto the rocks; up on your right the Old Town sticks out over the abyss like a seagull's nest. Drive along the Avenue Charles de Gaulle and park opposite the tourist office. Alternatively, make the dramatic entry via the fortress stairs. Far off, on the other side of the **Strait of Bonifacio**, the bluish, hazy coastline of Sardinia can be seen shimmering in the distance.

From the tourist office head into town via the **Monument Légion Étrangère**, which once used to stand in the North African town of Saïda. The Legion occupied the western side of the rock until 1983, and left it completely desolate. Follow the signs for **Escalier du Roi d'Aragon** (open daily 11am–5.30pm; admission charge). Legend has it that this stone staircase leading down to the sea, with its 187 steps, was carved out of the rock by soldiers from Aragon in just one night, but it existed long before that to give access to the well. From Place Monte Pagani continue along Rue Doria – you could

Bonifacio is perched on the cliffs

One way of getting around

gain another panoramic view from Tour du Bastardello − before heading to the town's main gate.

The fortifications begin above Saint-Roch, at the **Belvédère de la Manichella**. The Montée Saint-Roch leads to it through a drawbridge which provided the only means of access until well into the 19th century. On the harbour side the wall of the Citadel drops away steeply; it used to enclose the upper town as far as the round tower called the Torreone high above the sea. The inhabitants here were always well-equipped to withstand sieges − the one by the King of Aragon in 1420 lasted five months.

On Rue des Deux Empereurs you can explore the houses where Napoleon and Charles V stayed when stormy weather if not politics prevented them from leaving. The 14th-century church of **Sainte-Marie-Majeure** has a highly ornamental tower and also a loggia − a roofed courtyard with an arcade − where the city elders used to hold their meetings. Inside the church, a 3rd-century Roman sarcophagus made of marble once served as a font, and the tabernacle (1465) is also a rare treat. Now head back towards the tourist office and to the tip of the peninsula.

The round towers, recently restored, were once windmills; casemates and cannon emplacements were built close to the Genoese bastions. They now form part of an interesting walk along the top of the peninsula, the site of one of Bonifacio's most distinctive spectacles, the **Cimtière des Marins** (Sailors' Cemetery). Corsicans are renowned for their love of large-scale tombs and other funerary monuments, but this mini-town of domes, spires and ostentatious mausoleums is in a class of its own. You could easily spend an hour wandering through its lanes, admiring the quirky architecture and gazing out across the Strait to Sardinia. Next to the cemetery, the **Convent of St François** is believed to have been founded after St Francis of Assisi sheltered in a sea cave nearby. According to the story, a woman from the town accidentally emptied a pan of slops over his head, and the convent was Bonifacio's apology.

From the end of the promontory, a road skirts around its northern edge, providing views down to the harbour entrance and the **La Madonetta lighthouse**.

Back near the tourist office, **Saint-Dominique** can be seen with its octagonal tower and battlements. It is the only Gothic church on the island and very severe in style. Several *chasses* – processional figures carried around during Easter Week – are kept here.

Down on the **Quai Comparetti**, fishing boats and yachts lie anchored directly in front of a row of restaurants and cafés, with menus and snacks to suit every size of wallet. An **aquarium marin** (open daily 10am–8.30pm; admission charge), its contents supplied by the local fishermen, displays some of the marine life along this stretch of the coast. People even dive for red gorgonian coral here – it grows at depths of 60m (200ft) or more – and a craft enterprise at the bottom of the Montée Rastello uses it to make beautiful jewellery.

The boat trip to the enormous 'Grain of Sand' rock and the blue depths of the **Grotte du Sdragonatu** takes just over an hour. Give yourself a bit longer, though, if you want to visit the **Iles Lavezzi**, a beautiful archipelago composed of windswept and water-eroded rocks. In stormy weather this series of flattish cliffs can be absolute hell. The frigate **La Sémillante** was wrecked here in 1855 on its way to the Crimea. All 750 people on board perished. Victims who were washed ashore lie buried in three of the island's graveyards.

Follow the **footpath** leading from the Oratoire St Roch, just below the main entrance to the Haute Ville. It winds along the edge of Bonifacio's famous striated chalk cliffs, affording fine views across the straits and back towards the town itself. After a little under an hour, you'll reach the tip of the island at **Capo Pertusato**, crowned by a lighthouse from where the panorama extends over the islands of Cavallo and Lavezzi, as well as the northern shores of Sardinia.

9. Stones that Speak

A journey west from Bonifacio past natural rock formations, then back inland to Sartène and the primeval fortresses at Cucuruzzu and Capula. A side-trip to the megalithic site of Filitosa. See map opposite.

Just north of Bonifacio, the N196 branches to the left towards Sartène and Ajaccio. Very soon, over on the right you can see the **Uomo di Cagna**, an enormous boulder perched precariously at the very top of a 1,217-m (4,000-ft) high mountain. Whether formed by the elements or arranged by the hand of man, such fascinating stones and rock formations are a distinctive part of the Corsican landscape: in **Caldarello**, situated 1km to the south of the N196, the houses are scattered about in a great jumble of rocks. Of interest

The lion of Roccapina

Sartène

here are the hollowed-out caves and grottoes (*tafoni*). Long ago, people put windows and doors into the openings, and they were inhabited until as recently as the 17th century. Today they are used as stables and store-rooms.

After the small town of Pianotolli-Caldorello, at the top of a small pass, your gaze will be drawn to a weird rock formation straight ahead – the **Lion de Roccapina**. The beast seems to be enjoying a siesta on a rocky outcrop above the sea; a few kilometres further on, at the **Auberge Coralli**, a narrow, unsurfaced track leads down to the exquisite beach below the lion. From the end of the track, you can clearly see that its 'mane' is artificial, and is actually made up of the crumbling ruins of what once used to be a coastal fortress.

Another place that seems part of the rock it stands on is **Sartène** (Sartè), or at least its old town. This 'most Corsican of Corsican towns', as Prosper Mérimée, author of *Carmen* and *Colomba*, described it in 1839, has a relaxing square and atmospheric medieval core.

Parking is difficult. There is a large car park to the left of the incoming road (unmarked in this direction) just before the roundabout or a smaller one if you turn right at the roundabout. From the roundabout walk up U Corsu (ignoring the sign pointing to centre-ville – it is only to indicate the one-way system to drivers). Walk past the **Echauguette**, and after a brief ascent you'll find yourself in the town's shady central square, the **Place Porta**. Through a gate beneath the *mairie* (formerly the Genoese governor's palace), a few

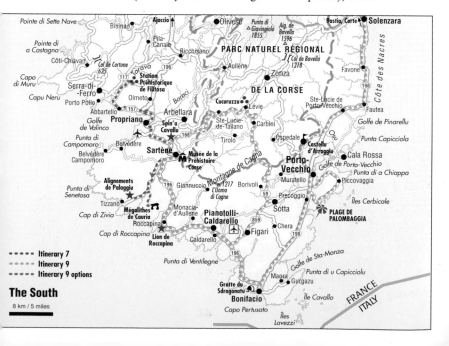

Itinerary 7
Itinerary 9
Itinerary 9 options

The South

8 km / 5 miles

A meeting of like minds in Sartène's main square

more steps will transport you into the medieval atmosphere of the **Manighedda Quarter**. The passages, alleyways and stone staircases here are almost entirely devoid of light, and run between houses built of rough slabs of masonry, some of them eight storeys high.

This dimly lit *Quartier* was the breeding-ground for the Vendetta. Drawn into the feuds between the all-powerful landowners, different neighbourhoods of the town would battle each other at the slightest provocation. It was only in 1834 that a contract signed in the church of **Santa-Maria** put an end to the fighting. This gruesome past also goes a long way towards explaining the rite of the **Catenacciu** – the name given to an anonymous penitent wearing a red cowl with slits for the eyes, with a 14-kg (31-lb) chain attached to his ankle, who on Good Friday shoulders a massive cross weighing 31kg (68lb) and carries it through the town barefoot *(see page 80)*.

Off to the right above the Place Porta, the **Musée de la Préhistoire Corse** (open daily except weekends 10am–noon and 2–5pm; admission charge) occupies a building adjacent to the da Prisa. If renovation work is complete on the new exhibition hall, you'll be able to look at finds from across the island, spanning 6,000BC to 500BC. A visit here will stand you in good stead for the afternoon.

At this point you can fortify yourself with a snack in one of the *brasseries* on the Place Porta or a proper lunch at the **Auberge A Tinedda** below the city, in the direction of Propriano. However, if you want to experience the highlight of this afternoon's trip – the Stone Age fortress at Cucuruzzu – in all its glory without anyone else around, it's best to have a picnic handy and to use this quiet time for travelling. Follow the road downhill out of Sartène in the direction of **Propriano** (Pruprià), turn off right after 6km (4 miles) along the D268. After about 3km (2 miles) you can stop briefly on the right at a lay-by to admire the elegance of the Genoese bridge known as the **Spin'a Cavallu** (horse's back) over the Rizzanese. About half an hour later you'll reach **Ste Lucie-de-Tallano**, and it's worth stopping briefly here, too, in the square with its war memorial, because the plinth of the statue is made of a stone that is very rare indeed: it is a type of diorite that can only be found in one private quarry on Corsica, and also in Finland: *diorit orbiculaire*.

Continue in the direction of Levie until you see a sign just after the Cumuna di Mela on the left, pointing the way towards the **Sites Archéologiques de Levie** at **Cucuruzzu** and **Capula**. After about 10 minutes the road ends in a car park. A small stone information booth points the way to the most fascinating primeval fortresses on the island, alongside Arraghju *(see page 41)*. Cucuruzzu is a 15-minute walk, Capula is 20 minutes more from there and it takes 15 minutes more to get back to your starting point. The path passes through bizarre rock formations and giant, moss-covered trees, the whole place like an enchanted forest.

Cucuruzzu was built around 1500BC, during the Bronze Age, on a natural rock formation. 'Parc Naturel' signs explain how the place was constructed. From the walls the view across to the **Aiguilles de Bavella** (1,596m/5,200ft) is superb. The site was abandoned in the 3rd century BC, but the Bronze Age fortress at Capula was extended several times and used as a refuge by the island's *signori* as late as the 13th century – which is why it looks so much more modern. More information is available in Levie. Backtrack to the D268 and follow the signs to Levie. The **Musée Archéologique** is straight ahead as you enter town (open daily except Sun, 10am–

An enchanted landscape

noon and 2–4.30pm; admission charge). The oldest lady in Corsica can be seen lying here too – in a coffin: the skeleton of the 'Lady of Bonifacio', who died 8,500 years ago aged 35. A 15th-century ivory crucifix of the Donatello School can also be seen here.

You can now take the D59 to **Carbini** with its free-standing campanile, visible for miles around. Built in the late 11th century, it is probably the oldest bell-tower on the island. The church of **San Giovanni** next to it is also Pisan. A rebellion began here in the 14th century: the sect of the Giovannali, who threatened the order of the church and the *signori* by demanding equality, were eventually accused of debauchery and put to death by papal soldiers inside the church. From Carbini you can then take the D59/859 past Sotta and via Figari, before rejoining the N196 to Bonifacio.

An alternative destination for the afternoon, particularly if you're heading to Ajaccio, is the megalithic site of **Filitosa** (open daily 9am–8pm, or until dusk; admission charge), home to the island's most impressive collection of statue-menhirs. From Sartène continue along the N196, drive around the outside of **Propriano** and then about 5km (3 miles) further on, where the N196 goes round a large hairpin, turn down to the left on to the D157 and travel along the coast in the direction of Porto Pollo. You'll notice the signs to Filitosa, which is situated on a slope above the broad valley of the Taravu.

The original inhabitants of the island, the Corsi, sculpted the statues in their own image and in the image of the ultimately victorious Torréen invaders. Only a few steps into the site, you're confronted by a grim-looking menhir-guard, armed with dagger and sword: this is a Torréen menhir. The menhir heads you come across next lined up in a row on the round wall of the central monument actually look the most peace-loving of the lot, and only a few fragments betray the odd breast-plate or weapon. These were probably ritual stelae created by the Corsi before the arrival of the Torréens. The invaders smashed them and used the fragments to help build their *torre*. The tower-like West Monument, high above the valley, was also used by the Corsi. Down below, further menhirs were also placed to form a partial circle. Seen from above they appear very lifelike, and reveal features very different from those of their 'colleagues' above.

There are more sculptures in the small museum just before the exit: **Scalsa Murta** (circa 1400BC) was found in very good condition; with its helmet and its muscular chest. The depressions in the helmets were probably there to accommodate cattle-horns.

Other statue-menhirs in the south of the island can be seen at the Alignements de Palaggiu and the Mégalithes de Cauria, both to the south of Sartène. They, too, represent the victors and the vanquished. Here though it was the Christians who used the statues as material to build their churches, after they had duly exorcised them.

If you have visited the site at Filitosa, I suggest you round off the day with a swim at **Abbartello**, directly opposite Propriano. Ajaccio is 75km (45 miles) away from here on the N196.

Among the menhirs of Filitosa

The West Coast

10. Ajaccio

From the morning market to Napoleon's birthplace and visits to
the Chapelle Impériale and the Musée Fesch. See map page 50.

In **Ajaccio** (Aiacciu) the regional parliament looks after politics and concentrates on lobbying the central government in Paris, which can make life rather hectic
at times. But above all else, Ajaccio is imbued with the
aura of the island's greatest son, **Napoleon**. It's less
of an aura these days – more like an enor-
mous neon sign. It's not only the statues and the historic sites, either:
apart from all the souvenir
kitsch, a cinema has been named
after him and he has even been
used to help market light bulbs,
which can be seen dangling
above the streets like Christmas decorations throughout the
entire year.

Napoleon with his brothers on the Place Diamant

The first thing you need to do
in this rather chaotic town is to find some relatively peaceful accommodation *(see page 91–2)*. If you're just passing through, parking is available beneath the **Place Diamant** (its real name is actually
Place de Gen de Gaulle), and at the harbour ferry in front of the market in the **Square César Campinchi**. From here you can reach all
the town's sights on foot.

The **morning market** (open daily except Mon, 6am–2pm) here is more
colourful and luxurious than its equivalent in Bastia. In the adjoining building complex, facing the sea, is the **fish hall**; the other side
of the same building faces the Place Foch and contains the Office de
Tourisme, the Town Hall and, on the first floor, a **Salon Napoléonien**
(open daily 9–11.45am and 2–5.45pm; admission charge). Here you
can see a marble statue of Jérôme Bonaparte, King of Westphalia,
wearing a Roman toga, pointing the way towards the *Grand Salon* with
its portraits and busts, Napoleon's birth certificate written in Genoese

Italian (a photocopy), and his death mask – another copy – cast in bronze – the original is in Paris. In the direction of the town centre, at the end of the Place Foch, beneath the plane trees and palms, you can see Napoleon himself as **Premier Consul** keeping an eye on the Four Lions Fountain. The small statue of the Virgin set into a façade across to the left, known as **A Madonnuccia**, is supposed to have protected the town from the plague in 1656; it certainly seems to have done more for Ajaccio than Napoleon ever did.

The Rue Bonaparte leads past this house on the corner and up towards the Citadelle (closed to visitors), and in the third street to the right you'll find **Napoleon's birthplace**, the **Casa Maison Bonaparte** (open Mon–Sat 9am–noon and 2–6pm, Sun 9am–noon; admission charge). Back in 1769 the building was by no means as elegant as it is now. Laeticia, Napoleon's *Madame Mère* from Sartène, only managed to do it up with the help of compensation after it had been virtually demolished by the British and the Paolists. In the small garden opposite you can see the bust of the Roi de Rome when he was still a child, the son of the Emperor and Marie-Louise of Austria. He was meant to become Napoleon II, but achieved fame as the Duke of Reichstadt. The sedan chair in the *entrée* to the Casa is the one Laeticia is supposed to have been carried home in from church when she felt her first labour pains – the furniture inside the building is even less authentic and altogether rather gaudy.

Something far closer to the average Corsican's heart can be found if you go up the Rue Saint-Charles a short way and go left and then right, to reach the cathedral of **Notre-Dame-de-la-Miséricorde**. Through the portal on the right, in a niche behind a small grating, you can see the font, and a red marble plaque on a pillar to the left attests to Napoleon's desire to be buried in his native

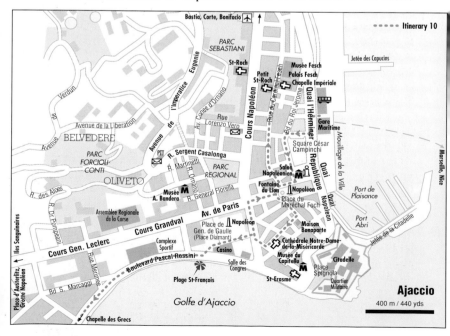

city. However, when he died on St Helena in 1821 he no longer belonged to his island; he was far too famous by then, and was buried not in the imperial tomb at Ajaccio, but under the dome of Les Invalides in Paris.

You will see Napoleon again, up on horseback this time, wearing golden laurels, staring across the Place Diamant and surrounded by four regal personages on foot: his brothers Joseph, Lucien, Louis and Jérôme. And at the end of the long avenue leading away from the Four Lions Fountain, you can see him yet again in one of his typical poses, with the fingers of his left hand thrust inside his jacket. The ramp proudly displaying all the names of his military victories is used today as a slide by children from the nearby blocks of flats. The young Bonaparte is meant to have played in a grotto at the back on the left.

The **Chapelle Impériale** (open Mon 1–5pm, Tues–Sun 9.15am–12.15pm and 2.15–5.15pm; admission charge) in the Rue Fesch contains the remains of his parents, a few family members and Cardinal Fesch, a stepbrother of Laeticia's, the art-loving archbishop of Lyons, who collected around 16,000 paintings, mostly by Italian masters. The chapel forms the south wing of the **Palais Fesch** (same hours as above; admission charge), in whose courtyard a bronze statue shows the cardinal with his hand placed on his heart. Although the ravages of time have left only about a thousand of his paintings in Ajaccio, these do make up what is considered to be the third most important collection of 14th–18th-century Italian works in the world, after those in the Uffizi in Florence and the Louvre in Paris. Among the works on display in the renovated building (opening hours vary, see *page 96*) are a triptych from the **Rimini School** and several paintings by Giotto, Botticelli, Bellini, Titian, Caravaggio and Veronese.

Napoleon's ramp

In the evening, why not do as Napoleon did while still a young man? He used to walk westwards as far as the **Chapelle des Grecs** along the Rue des Sanguinaires. Before or after enjoying an evening apéritif at one of the cafés on the seafront boulevard de Lantivy, depending on the time of year, you too can travel 12km (7½ miles) westwards to the **Pointe de la Parata** and watch the sun sink down behind the Iles Sanguinaires.

Beauty on the beach

11. Ajaccio to Porto

Deserted beaches, the Greek town of Cargèse, the Calanches Rocks and the Golfe de Porto, now under UNESCO protection. See map opposite.

Follow the N194 northeastwards out of Ajaccio. The quickest route to the north of the island and Calvi would involve continuing along the main road via the central mountains, Corte and L'Île Rousse – but that would mean missing out on the best and most spectacular part of the west coast, so I suggest you turn left at Mezzavia, after about 4km (2½ miles), following the sign which reads 'Calvi par la côte'.

Once you've entered Ajaccio's hinterland you can see the Golfe de Lava down below on the left, after which you reach the top of the pass known as the **Bocca di San Bastiano** (411m/1,350ft). Beyond it you can see the Cinarca rising above the Golfe de Sagone. Like the Balagne *(see Itineraries 13 and 14)*, the Cinarca, too, was once a very fertile landscape. Long after the arable land to the north *(Terra di u cummune)* had been partitioned equally and justly, the Cinarca was still under the yoke of the feudal *signori*. Its valleys facing the sea are now prospering economically, thanks to the tourist boom on the coast.

The first large bay you reach, the **Golfe di a Liscia** between Ancone and Tiuccia, is packed with holiday villas. This suddenly changes the moment you round the Genoese tower at the Punta di Capigliolo. The long, gently curving beach either side of the **Liamone Estuary** is still wild and unspoilt. Its first half is almost completely bare, and beyond the river it is bordered by an area of bush. Just the place for a longish morning swim, though when the wind gets the surf up the current here can get pretty dangerous. Nevertheless, Ajaccio's only about an hour behind you, and you can take your time. Sagone or Cargèse are good places for lunch, and neither is far away.

The coast road near Porto

The left turn out of Sagone will take you along the beach and at the end of this short, straight section of road on the right, just after you cross the bridge over the Sagone river, you'll see a near-ruin standing about 90m (300ft) away on the right. This used to be the 12th-century episcopal **Cathédrale of Sant' Appiano**. Its foundations are far older: they date from the 4th century. Directly above the site, a menhir can be clearly seen, acting as a cornerstone.

Cargèse lies a 15-minute drive to the west, and is situated high above the sea. It was founded by around 600 Greeks from the Peloponnese town of Vitylo, on the run from Turkish occupation. They first settled a bit further up the slope in 1676 and named their community Paomia. Their successful attempts at agriculture combined with their loyalty to Genoa, however, soon incurred the envy and the wrath of the Corsicans. In 1732 they were driven from their homes by the people living in the mountains near Vico. After suffering two periods of exile in Ajaccio, they were finally allowed home again for good in 1793 during the French occupation of the island.

Today, reminders of the area's Greek origins can be found in the surnames of the local population, many of which end in *-polis* or *-dacci* (from *-dakis*), and in the local white Greek Orthodox church. This stands opposite a very Corsican-looking church, constructed by members of the local parish in 1870, which contains a whole wealth of icons, some of them from Mount Athos. Mass here is celebrated by the same priest, who wears different raiments depending on which church he happens to be in.

The West Coast

8 km / 5 miles

- - - - **Itinerary 11**
- - - - **Itinerary 12**

Halfway to **Piana**, on a bend in the road beyond a bridge, a stele can be seen commemorating the island's liberation at the end of 1942. At a spot in the *maquis* further up the mountain, officers who had come ashore from the submarine *Casabianca* met leaders of the Corsican resistance movement for initial discussions, and distributed weapons.

The road now winds its way across uninhabited countryside, until you see the whole **Golfe de Porto** from the **Col de Lava** (498m/1,600ft) just before reaching Piana. This gulf, with its red porphyritic rocks, is now under UNESCO protection. Its most spectacular section begins suddenly at a bridge over a mountain stream beyond Piana: the **Calanches**. For years, Corsican shepherds called it a 'work of the devil': a rough and bizarrely shaped mass of rock with contours reminiscent of mythical creatures and monsters. You can reach some of these rock formations, the 'Eagle' or the 'Tortoise' for instance, by going up the path next to the bridge beyond the **Chalet des Roches Bleues**. Three-quarters of an hour later the path, quite steep at first, leads back to the main road. Further down, on a sharp curve, the hour-long alternative route heads off via the 'dog's head' *(tête de chien)* to a natural 'château' with a magnificent view across the whole Golfe de Porto.

Porto is guarded by its square tower

This area's finest panorama, however, is from the summit of **Capo d'Orto** (1,294m/4,245ft), the peak whose dramatic north wall rises sheer above Porto village. The mountain presents a less intimidating profile on its southern flank, where an easy, well-marked trail winds through aromatic pine forest and across uplands dotted with bizarre rock formations to the summit. It starts outside Piana, 1.5km (1 mile) along the D81 towards Porto (look for a rocky track peeling right off at a sharp bend in the road where there's a stone bridge). Free maps are available from Piana tourist office. The route takes around five hours to complete, there and back.

In the old days **Porto** used to be nothing more than a tiny fishing harbour belonging to the mountain village of **Ota**, situated 4½km (2½ miles) inland. Porto was one of the first places on the island to be developed into a tourist centre. UNESCO protection arrived rather late, but has ensured that the local red stone is used for all new housing projects so a natural atmosphere is retained. Once you've chosen a hotel for the night from the huge selection available, there's still time to go for a swim on the pebble beach in front of the eucalyptus grove. The water here sometimes bubbles like champagne.

A brief walk in the Gorges de Spelunca. Then two mountain passes with superb views across the Golfe de Girolata. See map on page 53.

The Genoese bridge at Ota

The Porto River flows through a whole series of torrents thundering down from the alpine watershed. The ones that have cut deepest into the rock here are the Tavulella and the Aïtone, forming the **Gorges de Spelunca**. The old mule track to the mountain village of Evisa passes through these gorges, and going uphill the whole way would take over three hours. However, a short walk in the lowest part of the gorge gives you a very good idea of what the island's former 'road system' was like.

First of all, drive to **Ota**. There are legends galore about the Sphinx-shaped rock high above the village: according to one of them, two monks up there have been restraining the rock for centuries with the aid of hemp ropes. On the other side of the village the road descends to the entrance to the gorge, and just before it on the right you can see a well-preserved Genoese bridge spanning the Porto River. The footpath into the gorge – part of the **Tra mare e monti** hiking trail – begins on the right at the double road bridge, and leads you alongside the mountain stream for 45 minutes until it reaches a second Genoese humpbacked bridge, the **Pont de Zaglia**, where the Tavulella and the Aïtone join forces. This is where you turn back.

Lunch or a picnic can be combined with a swim on the spectacular pebble beach at **Bussaglia**; roughly 5km (3 miles) to the north of Porto, a short side-road off the D81 will take you down there. After this you come to the section of road with more curves than anywhere else on this coastal route. Stop briefly at the **Col de la Croix**, 272m (890ft) above the Golfe de Girolata. The fort and several houses belonging to the village of **Girolata** can be seen from here. The village can be reached from the Col in around 90 minutes via an ancient mule track that winds downhill through dense *maquis* to a little cove, and then scales a second hill to reach the village. It's a popular walking route that has been

Snack on the Col de la Croix

made famous in recent years because of its association with local celebrity Guy the Postman, who jogs along it six times each week to deliver the mail. A couple of documentaries have been made about him, and bus tours now turn up to greet his arrival at the Col de la Croix. At Girolata itself, you can refuel at a couple of picturesque cafés and restaurants overlooking the beach. Alternatively, catch one of the daily pleasure boats that leave from Porto or Calvi.

In order to reach the **Col de Palmarella** on the opposite side – 4½km (2½ miles) as the crow flies – the road has to zig-zag its way 11½km (over 7 miles) along the slopes. The other pass is higher up (406m/1,300ft), and the view across the bay, framed by mountains, is unforgettable.

The road winds its way down quickly, around innumerable bends and through a lot of *maquis*, to reach the **Fango** valley. The riverbed here is usually dry. **Galéria**, a remote fishing port is thought to have been occupied since the 6th-century BC. Spread around a crescent-shaped bay and tiny boat jetty, the village lay all-but deserted until after World War II, when the American military sprayed its hinterland to rid the area of malaria-carrying mosquitos. Now it's a pretty little resort in summer, with a handful of cosy cafés, restaurants and guest houses. The coarse-sand beach is safe for swimming and there are some great walks into the hills, the best of them the six-hour trek to Girolata. This route, marked with orange paint blobs, offers some of the finest views of the west coast and Paglia Orba massif; you can follow it for four hours to reach the high point then turn around. It's only the valley's unusual width and the number of boulders on either side that betray the huge masses of water that crash through here when the snow thaws or during heavy rainstorms.

A stone bridge with five arches leads you to the other bank. Upriver, you can see the **Paglia Orba** *(see page 34)*, which looks a lot more like the Matterhorn from here than it did from the Niolo side. If you turn right here and travel inland on the D81 you can reach Calvi much more quickly. The left turn, though – the D81B – is a winding but beautiful coastal road. You pass two grey-sand and pebble beaches down below on the left; one opposite Galéria and the other at Argentella. And on a hill in front of the mountains, its windows empty and looking very solitary indeed, stands what is left of **Torre Mozza**. Not a watchtower, but instead the all-too-brief dream of a member of the Bonaparte family who was keen on the Romantic 'back-to-nature' movement.

13. Calvi

A stroll through the Citadel and the narrow streets beyond the quay. Lunch in the central square or down at the harbour. An afternoon excursion out into the Basse-Balagne. See map page 59.

I could spend hours in a wicker armchair outside a café on Calvi's Quai Landry, especially during the quiet months when the snow glistens high up on the massive Monte Grosso (1,938m/6,358ft) opposite – but I know that the view of the bay and the mountains is far finer from up in the **Citadelle**. Trot past the **Tour de Sel** beside the water and walk up to the fortress above. Over the gateway to it you can read *Civitas semper fidelis* – Calvi was always loyal to Genoa.

Citadel steps

From the first parapet, the cobblestones lead up and around to the **Place d'Armes**. On the left are the Sampiero barracks, formerly the governor's palace. On the other side of the street, a few steps beyond the row of facades, you can visit the **Oratoire de la Confrèrie Saint-Antoine** with its exhibitions of religious art (only open May–Sept).

Constructed according to a cruciform ground plan in the 13th century, and restored in the 18th century, the church of **Saint-Jean-Baptiste** is surprisingly bright inside because of its lantern. On the left as you go in there are several old marble fonts, and if you carry on in a clockwise direction, you'll see a fine filigree tabernacle of dark wood in the first niche you come to, surrounded by some very ornate processional crosses. Go up a couple of steps, and inside a glass case there is a fine wooden madonna from Seville (1757) known as the **Virgin of the Rosary**. The figure is normally dressed in light blue, but during the Easter week processions through the town, she wears black and, later, gold brocade.

The altar itself (16th century) is a masterpiece of intarsia work with polychrome marble. Behind it, among various

The Citadel

The harbour at Calvi

busts of the clergy, is a triptych (1498) by the Ligurian artist Barbagelata. In the gap you can see the church's patron saint, John the Baptist, standing behind a group showing St Nicholas with children, probably carved locally. On the right of the altar stands a **Christ des Miracles**, which is said to have brought an end to the Turkish siege in 1553. In the direction of the entrance on both sides, above the richly carved chancel, you can see the special boxes, with access from the outside, that were used by the town's wealthy families.

Flights of steps and various passageways lead past the church to the external fortifications. From the **Teghjale corner bastion** there's a superb view of both the bay and the Golfe de Revellata. In 1794, debris scattered by a shot fired from these very battlements struck Lord Nelson's right eye, destroying his sight; he had come ashore to assist with the capture of the town.

Nearby, a sign designates one of the houses ruined by Nelson's siege as 'The Birthplace of Christopher Columbus'. It's a contentious claim based on rather tenuous evidence, but that hasn't stopped the local municipality from declaring 12 October, the explorer's supposed birthday, as a public holiday.

Down below, between the Boulevard Wilson and the Boulevard Clemenceau, you'll find all the holiday shopping you could possibly wish for. The *piazza* in front of the church of **Sainte-Marie-Majeure** is a good place for lunch and supper, and narrow passageways also lead back down to the Quai Landry with its huge assortment of bars, brasseries and restaurants. Then comes the flat expanse of beach, backed by even more bars and cafés.

Virgin of the Rosary

On the other side of the bay, in front of the mountains and a short distance inland, you can make out the small village of **Montemaggiore**. It's the first stop on your afternoon tour northwards into the **Basse-Balagne**. Leave Calvi on the N197, passing the turn-off to the airport of Sainte-Cathérine (Santa Catalina), and soon afterwards turn right towards Calenzana on the D151, which you follow for only a few hundred metres before turning left on to the D451. Montemaggiore is beautifully situated on a rocky outcrop, and the church square offers a fine view of the gulf below. This village has a historic link with a man most people consider either a legend or an opera character – Don Juan. The family tree of an old established local family proves that famous ladies' man Don Miguel de Leca y Colona y Magnara y Vincentello, born in Seville, Spain in 1627, actually had his family roots back here in Montemaggiore.

Montemaggiore

From the church square the D151 goes off to the left to L'Île Rousse, and the view of Calvi and its bay from this road is the most breathtaking so far. The road finally reaches its highest point at the **Col de Salvi** (509m/1,670ft). At the crossroads in Cateri you then continue straight on and soon afterwards go up to the right, to **Sant'Antonino**. This village is just like an eagle's nest, perched on a ridge between two steep valleys, between the mountains and the sea. It dates back to the 9th century.

A good place to park is down on the left next to the church, and at this point don't be distracted by the flight of steps going straight up to the square, but instead walk off to the left and go up around the edge of the village. Of course you could be even more true to style, and hire a donkey at the car park: all the typically wide and gently sloping steps in these Corsican villages were built to accommodate the *pas d'âne* ('donkey's pace'). Suddenly you'll find yourself in a *loghja*, or *corps de passage* – a series of vaulted passageways with lots of corners, leading to an enchanted little square with a chapel, before heading up to the highest houses

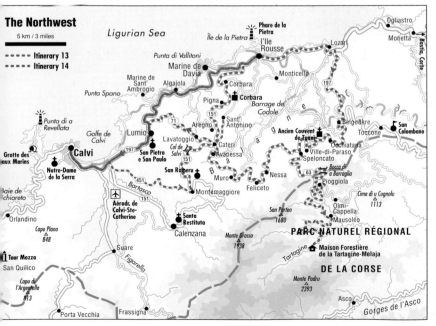

Detail of the Trinity Church

in the village. Fine view follows fine view, until the path finally takes you back to the church once again.

Rejoining the D151, turn sharp right and drive down in the direction of **Aregno**. Before you get there you pass the **Pisan Church of the Trinity** (1177) in its small graveyard, also consecrated to John the Baptist. Its warm, yellowish-brown stone forms a fine counterpart to the green-and-white of San Michele in Murato. The church has no tower, but take a close look at the figure below the gable: isn't it in the process of removing a thorn from its foot? The figure stands above four arches with varying types of decoration, supported by five animal statues. The two figures above the portal seem also to have been drawn directly from everyday life – a farmer and his wife, perhaps? Or a monk and a shepherd?

Pigna is the next village as you head closer towards the sea. Artistic traditions have been revived here ever since the 1960s: long-forgotten musical instruments have been recreated and old Renaissance songs are being rediscovered. Signposts point the way to the workshops and sales rooms of the **Corsicada**, and in the **Casa Musicale**, after dinner on the terrace, *lamentu* and *paghjella* (typical song styles) are also offered on Tuesday nights during peak season. You can also stay the night here or, if you prefer, in the monastery above the next village, **Corbara**.

From there it is just 5km (3 miles) to **L'Île Rousse** (Isula Rossa), the town named after the red cliffs in its harbour. It was founded in 1758 by Pasquale Paoli in order to disrupt the supply route between Genoa and Calvi. Guarded ceremoniously by four palm trees, Paoli's bust gazes across a generously proportioned square, situated right next to the beach. To end the day, how about a quick *pastis* outside my local, the **Café des Platanes**? The drive back to Calvi from here, via Algajola and Lumio, only takes around half an hour.

The Café des Platanes

A whole row of ancient villages stretches across the Haute-Balagne like a string of pearls. Towering behind them are the northern peaks of the alpine massif. See map on page 59.

Following the route taken by the tour buses, you could see the Haute-Balagne in a morning or afternoon by travelling along its central corniche. But with so many villages and so many superb views it would be a shame not to visit the area beyond the mountain ridges, which is so mysterious that a whole day can go by in a flash. As with

the previous day's excursion to the Basse-Balagne, leave Calvi in the direction of Bastia, but this time pass the turn-off to Calenzana and carry straight on past the Foreign Legion barracks, Camp Raffali.

The N197 takes you towards **Lumio** (Lumiu). Just before the village, on the right, you'll see the Chapel of **San Pietro e San**

Goats are bred for their milk

Paolo. Turn right at the barrel with *'Vin'* written on it and park beside the cemetery. This 11th-century Pisan structure was probably built on the foundations of a Roman temple to Apollo or Mercury.

On the outskirts of the village, just off the main highway, be sure not to miss Christian Moretti's fascinating **knife forge** (open Mon–Sat 2.30–6.30pm), where blades are made using local iron ore mined and smelted according to traditional Corsican methods. A video outlines the process and you can watch the smiths at work most days.

Just after Lumio, turn right and follow signs to Lavatoggio and Belgodère on the D71. This is where the **Corniche de la Balagne** begins, the mountain road that passes through 10 villages and leads to five others, hugging the slopes and remaining at an altitude of around 300m (1,000ft) all the way.

Once you've passed the junction at Cateri, it's worth stopping at the next major bend in the road to admire the olive trees above the little village of **Avapessa**, some of which are nearly 1,000 years old. The mountain streams that flow under the corniche here from November to May run into the Codole reservoir at the bottom of the valley, and there's a waterfall at the bridge beyond **Muro** (Muru) that has cut deep into the rock. The massive baroque church in Muro contains a crucifix dating from 1659 that is supposed to possess miraculous powers: it failed to stop an accident in 1778, though, when the church roof fell in and killed 60 people.

Ville-di-Paraso

The same goes for **Feliceto** (Felicetu), which lies beneath the 1,700-m (5,600-ft) massif formed by San Parteo and Cima Caselle. Behind the church on the right, a glass-blower has a workshop *(verrerie)* and you can watch him at work on Monday, Wednesday and Friday. At the exit to the village, next to the bridge over the Regino, the millstones of the **Auberge U Mulinu** crush the olives every spring in time-honoured fashion to produce a fruity, high-quality oil – a technique that has mostly been superseded now by modern methods.

Nessa consists of just a handful of houses and a leafy square – it can be reached via a side road which then leads back to the main road again. A short while later the D663 branches up to the right off the D71 in the direction of **Speloncato** (Speluncatu).

At a height of 550m (1,800ft) above sea-level, the road comes out into a square resembling an opera set. There's a fountain splashing away happily in the middle, where the inhabitants fill their mugs and plastic bottles with clear mountain spring water before mealtimes. Near a church, the **Hotel Spelunca** has set up quarters inside the former private palace of Cardinal Savelli, who served as secretary of state to Pope Pius until 1864. The cardinal's nickname, *il cane corso* ('the Corsican dog') betrays both the amount of influence he wielded and the amount of popularity he enjoyed. A few steps further on, the **Collegiate church** contains a real treasure: its organ (1810), which, despite having suffered a few 'practical' alterations over the years, has now been fully restored, and sounds superb. Concerts are held in San Michele between the end of June and the beginning of July – also as part of the *Festivoce* series *(see pages 79–81)*.

Both 'Speluncatu' and 'Spelunca' are derived from the Corsican word for the grottoes, *spelunce*, above which the town was built and which served formerly as sheep pens or even as refuges from the Moors. Anyone who's worked up an appetite at this point can enjoy a simple snack at either of the two bistros in the square, while gazing out at everyday village life, or sample more refined local cuisine at the **Auberge de Domalto** (tel: 04 95 61 50 97), 6km (4 miles) down the hill on the D71.

Between the U Fanale restaurant and the church, the D63 to Olmi Capella weaves up a bare mountain slope. There's a good view of Speloncato below – and up at the top, at the **Bocca di a Barraglia** (1,099m/3,604ft), you have the entire Balagne at your feet. The view stretches from the Punta di a Revellata beyond Calvi, past the rocks off L'Île Rousse with their lighthouses and the beaches at Lozari and Ostriconi, all the way to the Désert des Agriates near the Cap Corse.

If you turn to face the other side of the pass, you'll see Monte Padru (2,393m/7,850ft), the northern pillar of the mountain range. Beneath this huge mountain, the road now descends into an almost completely green valley, so near and yet so far from the tourist world of the coast. Ancient, gnarled oak-trees cast their shade on the asphalt, and in **Pioggiola**, the first hamlet you come to, the **Auberge L'Aghjola** is a good place to stop and eat – as is the equally Corsican but rather inconspicuous **Auberge La Tornadia** about 2km (1 mile) further on. The menus here feature baby trout, fresh from the sparkling mountain streams at the foot of Monte Padru.

After lunch, take the road that bears to the right towards **Tartagine**. Beyond the bridge there's parking at Tartagine's dilapidated but beautiful forest lodge. You'll have to clamber either up or down river a bit here, but soon you'll find your very own rockpool with its clear water, still refreshingly cool even at the very height of summer.

Some superb hiking paths extend from here into the heart of the Corsican watershed, whose peaks encircle the valley to the south. The classic route is a 5-hour circular walk that begins by following the river and then climbs to the village of **Mausoleo**; from here it drops back down to the wild Melaja Valley, crosses a stream, then follows the road back to the forest lodge. Leaflets describing the itinerary in detail are available at local tourist offices.

At the square in Speloncato with its fountain, turn right down to **Ville-di-Paraso** (Parasu). Have a stroll through the vaulted passageways below the narrow main street and look at the restored parish church surrounded by pompous but dilapidated tomb-chapels. This is a scene typical of pre World War I paintings by Maurice Utrillo and his mother Suzanne Valadon. Sadly, almost all of their paintings have disappeared from the area. They then lived in **Belgodère** (Belgudé).

The coast at Lozari

The corniche of the Haute-Balagne stops here, and once you've passed the church, the journey back down to the coast takes only around a quarter of an hour.

Shopping

Corsica is officially a part of France, after all, so you don't only see the usual cheap holiday rags dangling in the vaulted cellars of the coastal towns – formerly used for storing wood – but also a great deal of haute couture straight from Paris. Alta Moda creations from neighbouring Milan are a lot more rare – one of the reasons why the Italian women who shop here tend to buy Parisian chic. For those in search of such attire, a leisurely look around the fashion shops here is definitely to be recommended.

A typical grocery

There's always a shop open somewhere, except on Sunday afternoons – and in holiday centres in peak season they stay open even then. Corsica's small village shops are actually open for a few hours every day of the week throughout the year – but they also tend to be on the expensive side because of having to mark up their goods to cover the extra cost of transport from the mainland. Such establishments are good for putting together a nice picnic lunch. You'll find home-grown tomatoes here, dark red and incredibly delicious, unlike the half-ripe variety the supermarkets down by the coast tend to stock. Or you might find a sausage smoked by your *epicière*'s brother-in-law that's a mouldy grey on the outside but very tasty on the inside. Keep an eye out for sweet chestnut-flour biscuits, too, made according to local recipes. In fact the only thing you might find it hard to get hold of is bread, because the nearest baker sometimes lives a few villages away and a close count is thus kept on the loaves.

Island style, not always the height of fashion

Buy your herbs at the morning market

Markets

Every day except Monday, from the crack of dawn, Ajaccio and Bastia have their morning markets at which you can buy fruit and veg, smoked meats, pastries, herbs and spices, cheese, honey, olive oil and wine. Fish is also sold in the neighbouring halls and shops. In the island's smaller villages you'll find the whole assortment among the pillars of a *marché couvert* (covered market, or 'les halles'). If the day's catch has been particularly good, you'll have no problem buying the produce straight off the boat. At weekly markets – which irrationally tend to take place fortnightly – everyday clothing is sold, as are household goods for the local population, including cassettes of Corsican music (usually heard in the background), junk, old postcards, and – in summer – jewellery and local crafts. The *forains* (market stallholders) travel from town to town. Other very local markets feature regional goods, and it's at these, as well as at the different regions' annual markets, that real bargains can be found.

Arts and Crafts

Even on an island with deeply rooted craft traditions, there's quite a bit of kitsch around too, just as you'd expect. Of course if you don't mind, then a piece of horrid porcelain festooned with pictures of Napoleon might be just the souvenir for you. The island's serious artisans can usually be found in the shops bearing the names **Casa di L'Artigiani** or **Casa Paesana**. Here you will find a high-quality assortment of ceramics, baskets, Corsican woollen *(lana corsa)* pullovers and shawls, olive-wood carvings, baskets made from split chestnut branches or olive shoots, leather goods, painted silk, small sculptures and sketches, and even dried *maquis* in ceramic jars. Individual artisans, especially potters *(potiers)*, also signpost the way to their studios, which are often in remote villages and hard to find. Some studios proudly bear the **Corsicada** seal of quality – it originated in Pigna, a centre of traditional arts and crafts in the Lower Balagne, not far from L'Île Rousse. *Diorit orbiculaire* is a form of diorite that can only be found in one private quarry on Corsica (in the village of Ste-

The hallmark of quality

Lucie-di-Tallano), and also in Finland. Small polished sections of this mineral with its interesting feldspar rings, also known as corsite, can be bought at several souvenir shops on the island.

Antiques

The village houses belonging to old established families are treasure-troves full of old, simply made furniture and household objects, which are kept more for practical reasons than as status symbols. Typical are the *madia*, a trunk made of carved chestnut or lariciu pine, used to protect flour and bread from rats and field-mice, and the *bancu* (bench). You'll hardly ever see these marvellous old pieces of wooden furniture in the shops, though. Stores advertising *Brocante* or *Antiquitées* mostly contain wares from more recent times or other parts of France, though some of them do stock decorative tools found in the barns of remote villages.

Souvenirs from the sea

Food and Drink

The earliest islanders were hunters, gatherers and collectors, and their expertise has been handed down through generations, thus guaranteeing the quality of Corsican meat, cheese and honey. The pigs here roam freely, and are more closely related to their wilder and hairier relatives than most. The veal and beef doesn't contain any fast-growth hormones either. Nearly every village has its own secret recipe for ham *(prisuttu)*, lean steak *(lonzu)* or streaky bacon *(coppa)*. *Figatelli* is the name given to the strong-tasting mixture of liver-sausage and blood-sausage, toned down with herbs, which Corsicans love to roast over the fire and then eat with a slice of white bread. Wild boar, pigeon and blackbird *(merle)* pâtés are spiced with *nepita* (myrtle), a herb that tastes like a cross between mint and marjoram. Honey ranges from light to almost black, and the taste can be anything from light orange-blossom to dark and bitter-sweet *maquis*. Citrus fruits, kiwi, peaches, nuts, watermelons and blackberries are all used to flavour the island's different aperitif wines (most of them 15 percent alcohol), and the range of fruit and herb liqueurs is also huge.

People always used to say that the only wine Corsica produced was a very strong *vin ordinaire*. Most of the former cheap and high-yield vineyards have disappeared now, though, and Corsica's wine-makers are producing some fine-tasting wines from grapes suited to the sunny climate. The *Nielucciu* grape gives you a deep-red wine with a strong bouquet; *Sciacarellu* is lighter and a lot fruitier; and the *Vermentinu* grape forms the basis for the island's dry whites. Each of the nine AOC regions also produces a fresh rosé. The naturally sweet *muscat* wines from the Cap Corse and Patrimonio are drunk as aperitifs and dessert wines right across the island.

Eating Out

Although foreign tourists have been bringing their own eating habits to the island for a few decades now, French and therefore Corsican restaurants have remained faithful to the old menu pattern of *hors d'oeuvres,* main dish, cheese and then dessert. There's sometimes another course too, and you'll usually be asked if you'd like an aperitif when you're handed the menu. All this might be all right for the evening, but for most tourists it's an expensive and time-consuming way of spending one's lunchtime – with the result that many seats in the restaurants remain empty. The ubiquitous pizzeria is one way out of the situation, but in the beach cafés, too, nobody will mind if you take a break between sunning yourself and surfing to order a mixed plate *(assiette mixte)*, a colourful salad *(crudités)* or the dish of the day *(plat du jour)* with a drink.

Cuisine corse is simple, delicious and extremely filling – though in tourist areas it's not all that varied. The meal almost always starts with a selection of cold meats *(charcuterie)*, followed by a minestrone-like *soupe corse* or a fish soup containing croutons and *rouille*, a delicious spicy mayonnaise with saffron and garlic. For the main course there's often *boeuf corse* or *sauté de veau*, beef or veal stew with olives and mushrooms, or lamb *(agneau)*. Then there's local

sheep or goat's cheese varying from mild to strong, and to round off the meal, thinly sliced apple cake, or cheesecake with a squeeze of lemon. This last dish, known as *fiadone* or, more rarely, *embrucciata*, contains one of the most delicious specialities: *brocciu*. Sheep or goat's milk is added to the whey after the cheesemaking process and rises to the surface when heated. The foam is then spooned off and placed into baskets, where it achieves ricotta-like consistency. In desserts it is not only found in *fiadone* but in many other pastries, and sometimes it is eaten on its own with a dash of *eau-de-vie*. On the savoury side it is used in omelettes, and as a filling for cannelloni and trout.

Café in Saint-Florent

Fresh Fish

The trout on Corsica either come straight from the island's mountain streams, or from fish farms fed by mountain rivers. Salt-water fish only get caught by the local fishermen, unless strong winds prevent them from getting out in their tiny boats. Red mullet *(rouget)* or tuna-fish slices are grilled, but most typical of the island is the oven *('au four')* preparation of whole fish such as *chapon* (red weaver), *daurade* (gilthead) or *denti* (a type of perch), where the fish are baked on a bed of onions, tomatoes, fennel and herbs. *Denti* is also delicious when eaten cold with mayonnaise. There are no shrimps or prawns in Corsican waters, but lobster and spider-crab, *araignées*, squid *(calamares* and *seiches)* and octopus *(poulpes)* can all be found. On top of that, the mussels from the lagoons of Diane and Urbino on the east coast are fresh all year round. And in the cool season there are oysters too.

Marseilles is a Corsican bridgehead, and thus it's no wonder that the legendary *bouillabaisse* has also become part of the island's cuisine. The Corsicans call their version *aziminu*, and the compulsory ingredients include *rascasse* (a type of stickleback), *vive* (John Dory), *Saint-Pierre* and all manner of small crustaceans for the broth. It becomes *Royal,* and also particularly expensive, when rock-lobster gets added too. The odd bistro along the coast will also serve you *ormeaux* (stuffed mussels), and from the end of September sea-urchins *(oursins)*, too, are eaten with wine and bread.

Age-old Recipes

The family-run restaurants in the mountain villages often have no written menu and you may sometimes find yourself being served with a dish that's been cooked according to an almost forgotten recipe, handed down orally from generation to generation. Instead of the usual assortment of cold meats, for instance, there's *misgiscia* – salted and smoked pieces of mutton and goat's meat. A very traditional main course is chestnut *pulenda* (polenta), roasted in slices with *cabri* (young kid) in a rich sauce. Or *sturzapreti*, spiced dumplings topped with baked cheese consisting of *brocciu*, spinach and eggs. In the winter you may also find wild boar *(sanglier)*, quail *(cailles)* or young partridge *(perdreaux)*. Then for pudding there's *pisticcine*, a small cake made from chestnut flour, or *migliacce*, a kind of *tortilla* made from *brocciu*.

Corsican Wines

The lowest wines in the French hierarchical list are *vins de pays* and *vins de table*, both of them clean and strong-tasting and served in a *pichet*, or clay jug. The next level up is VDQS *(Vin Délimité de Qualité Supérieure)*, i.e. a good wine from a certain area. As far as the top classification, AOC *(Appellation d'Origine Contrôlée)*, is concerned, the state wine institute (known as INAO) controls the origin of the wine and sets a limit on the amount that can be produced per hectare in the respective region. A winemaker keen on quality will thus not only make sure he keeps his harvest below this limit, he will also press his grapes with the greatest possible care to produce the finest wine his soil can provide. Some vintners produce two AOC wines simultaneously. The *Clos Reginu* in the Balagne, for instance, not only produces the fine wine of the same name but also an even better one – red, white and rosé – with the suffix *E Prove*. It was once the sole preserve of the priesthood. Top Corsican white wines include *Clos Nicrosi* from the Cap Corse, Orenga de Gaffory's *Blanc de Blancs* from Patrimonio, and the *Torraccia* from the region around Porto-Vecchio. Among the reds, the light wines of Patrimonio, the *Fiumicicoli* from Sartène and also *Clos Capitoro* and *Comte de Peraldi* from the Ajaccio area are particularly famous.

Restaurants

Mealtimes are just as sacred to the Corsicans as they are to the French. Lunch lasts from noon–2pm: before and after that time there is scarcely any restaurant service available anywhere. The beach establishments are an exception to the rule though, and so are the snack bars, which will serve you *à toute heure* (around the clock) with a Corsican-style snack known as a *spuntinu*. Supper very rarely begins before 7.30pm – though it does get served slightly earlier during the tourist season – and the most crowded time of the evening is between 9pm and midnight, when the French and Italians, both used to eating late, squabble over the last few chairs. An aperitif is a good way of biding your time at this stage: a *pastis* – the Corsican brand is called *Casanis* – or a *Cap Corse* which is made up from wine, herbs and quinine. Naturally, every waiter will be familiar with that French invention, the *kir* – white wine with a dash of blackcurrant liqueur – or the *Kir Royal*, the same thing with champagne instead of wine. Regular customers – and some *patronne* will treat you as one after only your second visit – are offered an *apéro*, or a *digestif* after the meal, free of charge.

Good cooks on Corsica tend to come and go – not surprising, really, when you consider that the restaurants here are only properly packed for four months in the year. Only very few of them succeed in maintaining their reputation year after year. The following list is a choice of establishments that you will find along the itineraries I have suggested. Unless otherwise stated, the price ranges apply to the cheapest menus without wine. The à la carte prices are considerably more expensive: € = Budget under €25; €€ = Moderate €25–40; €€€ = Expensive €40 and up.

Bastia

A CASARELLE
6 rue Ste-Croix
Tel: 04 95 32 02 32
Serves delicious Balagne specialities, among which the *casgiate* (lumps of fresh ewe's cheese baked in a wrap of chestnut leaves) have earned the chef island-wide acclaim. This is the most appealing budget option in the Citadelle. **€**

LA CITADELLE
6 rue du Dragon, Citadelle
Tel: 04 95 31 44 70
French gourmet restaurant that's a shade more sophisticated, in both cuisine and atmosphere, than the competition, yet offers good value for money. *Magret de canard à l'orange* is the keynote dish, available *à la carte* only. **€€€**

U TIANU
4 rue Rigo
Tel: 04 95 31 36 67
Bastia holds few restaurants serving the *cuisine de campagne* that would have typified villagers' diets in the past – blackbird terrine, mutton and lentil stew and stuffed sardines – and this is the best of them. The restaurant is housed in a crumbling Genoese tenement down a narrow alley just behind the Vieux Port. **€€**

Cap Corse
Albo

CHEZ MORGANTI
Tel: 04 95 37 85 10
Famous seafood restaurant, in a building that was Cap Corse's first hotel. You can sit under a tamarind tree on a lovely terrace facing a little chapel, with a view over the harbour. Try their wonderful fish soup *capcorsine*. **€€**

Port Centuri

A MACCIOTTA (CHEZ SKER)
Behind the harbour
Tel: 04 95 35 64 46
Seafood aficionados shouldn't pass up the chance to eat at this tiny restaurant in a converted fisherman's cottage. Sea bass, anenomes and lobster feature on the showcase *menu poisson*. **€€**

Rogliano

AUBERGE SANT'AGNELLU
Bertolacce
Tel: 04 95 35 40 59
A gorgeous *terasse panoramique* surveys Macinaggio's beautiful hinterland. Here you can enjoy genuine hospitality and fine local cuisine. Most of the produce is gathered from the patron's brother's farm and you can taste the freshness. **€€**

Erbalunga

LE PIRATE
Off the square in the old quarter
Tel: 04 95 33 24 20
Cap Corse's flagship seafood restaurant, with a resolutely gastronomic menu that, unusually, caters well for vegetarians. **€€**

Dining at Calvi's Quai Landry

The Nebbio

Murato

FERME-AUBERGE CAMPU DI MONTE
3km (2 miles) below the village
Tel: 04 95 37 64 39
This is one of Corsica's most highly rated *ferme-auberges*, hidden away at the bottom of a valley below Murato (turn left at Victor Bar in the village and follow the signs). The proprietor, Mme Juillard, modestly attributes her success to the excellent quality of the locally sourced ingredients, recipes refined over three generations, and the magnificent location. **€€**

St-Florent

LA GAFFE
On the harbour front
Tel: 04 95 37 00 12
Classic seafood cuisine, based on produce from the gulf and restocked fresh each day. By far the best place to eat in this price bracket. **€€**

LA RASCASSE
On the harbour front
Tel: 04 95 37 06 99
Fashionable terrace restaurant on the marina with an inventive gourmet menu dominated by fish and crustacea: try their cream of scorpion fish, lobster sautéed in Nebbio *charcuterie* or mussel and *brocciu* fritters. **€€€**

LA ROYA
Plage de la Roya
Tel: 04 95 37 00 40
La Roya is one of very few restaurants on the island staking a serious claim to a Michelin star, hence its Pantagrualesque *menu prestige*, with its ultra-fancy interpretations on local standards (for example, 'spider crab turnover with a squirt of Scotch'). **€€€**

Castagniccia

A Porta

'CHEZ ELIZABETH' (AKA RESTAURANT DE L'AMPUGNANI)
Centre of the village
Tel: 04 95 39 22 00
Magnificent views and quality Castagniccian food, served in a larger and more impersonal dining hall in the region's main village. **€**

Campana

RESTAURANT SANT'ANDRIA
Tel: 04 95 35 82 26
Airy, wood-lined family restaurant, fitted with traditional carved furniture, overlooking the heart of the region. The *patronne* does the cooking herself, with Swiss chard and mint from the garden, pork reared in the local woods and tangy Niolo cheeses; and her chestnut desserts are a dream. **€**

Pedicroce

LE REFUGE
East of the village centre
Tel: 04 95 35 82 65

After the summer crush

Relaxation at the harbour front

Clinging to the side of the valley above a sea of woodland, this is the most obvious pitstop on the route through Castagniccia, at roughly the midway point. Chestnut and free-range pork and game dishes feature prominently on the various menus. €

Cervione

LES TROIS FOURCHETTES
In the village square
Tel: 04 95 38 14 86
Cosy budget restaurant just below a medieval *placette*, offering a 4-course menu of Castagniccian standards at an unbeatable price. €

Corte and the Niolo
Corte

U MUSEU
Rampe Ribanelle/rue Colonel-Feracci
Tel: 04 95 61 08 36
Reliable and efficient budget restaurant occupying a glass-sided building and terrace crouched below the Citadelle walls. U Museu offers a wide range of inexpensive *menus fixes*, and *à la carte* options including an enormous hot goat's cheese salad. €

AU PLAT D'OR
Place Paoli
Tel: 04 95 46 27 16
The only fine dining restaurant in town: its limited menu features typical *cortenais* dishes such as stuffed Tavignano trout in Cap Corse liqueur and beef bruschettas with wild morel mushrooms. €€

Calacuccia

AUBERGE DU LAC
Sidossi, 3km (2 miles) up the valley
Tel: 04 95 48 02 73
Sunny dining hall on the shore of the lake where you can sample top-grade *cuisine nioline*: pungent local cheeses, several kinds of *charcuterie* and succulent shepherds' stews. €€

The South
L'Etang de Diane

LE PIEDS DANS L'EAU
2km (1 mile) north of Cateraggio/Aléria
Tel: 04 95 57 04 55
Raised on stilts above the lagoon, this is the place to sample Aléria's legendary *nustale* oysters. They also do a delicious terrine made from dried

mullets' eggs, said to have been a local speciality since the time of the Romans. €€

Porto-Vecchio

LE TOURISME
In the Citadelle, opposite the church
Tel: 04 95 70 06 45
Refined French-influenced Porto-Vecchien cooking that's lighter and more imaginatively presented than the competition. Try their pasta dish of the day in mussel-and-pastis or wild asparagus sauce; and for dessert they do a divine chilled myrtle and strawberry 'soup'. €€

A CANTINA DI L'ORIU
5 cours Napoleon
Tel: 04 95 70 26 21
The region's finest artisanal *charcuterie*, cheeses, oils, olives and wines sampled in various *formules* in a stone-vaulted cave in the old quarter. €

Bonifacio

STELLA D'ORO (CHEZ JULES)
23 rue Doria, near the church of St-Jean-Baptiste
Tel: 04 95 73 03 63
This is the place to sample Bonifacio's showpiece dish, *merrizzane* – aubergine stuffed with *brocciu,* tomatoes and herbs, baked in a wood oven.

It's offered *à la carte*, alongside such delicacies as pasta in crayfish sauce. €€

CANTINA DORIA
27 rue Doria
Tel: 04 95 73 50 49
Simple regional dishes (including particularly tasty *lasagna à la bonifacienne*) served in a suitably rustic, vaulted dining room or on little tables out in the alley. Restrained prices for the Citadelle, and the wine list features the cream of southern Corsica's output. €

MARINA DI CAVU
Cala Longa, 6km (4 miles) out of town
Tel: 04 95 73 14 30
The last word in *haute gastronomie corse*, which you can enjoy in a swish dining hall moulded around a huge granite boulder and open fireplace, or on a magnificent poolside facing the Lavezzi Islands. €€€

Propriano

L'HIPPOCAMPE
Rue Jean-Pandolfi
Tel: 04 95 76 11 01
Top seafood from the gulf, served in simple surroundings at reasonable prices – a far safer choice than the row of more scenically situated restaurants lining the marina. €

Sartène

A TINEDDA
5km (3 miles) northwest along the Propriano road
Tel: 04 95 77 09 31
This is a down-to-earth *ferme-auberge* that offers a single set menu of wholesome and tasty local dishes – including the local speciality, *sweetbreads à la sartenaise* – in a snug dining room in winter or on a garden terrace in summer. Advance booking is essential. €

Corsica's refreshing chestnut beer

Levie

A PIGNATA
*5km (3 miles) west of Levie near Cu-
curuzzu archaeological site*
Tel: 04 95 78 41 90
Patronne Lily de Rocaserra is the long-
time standard bearer of Alta Roccan
cooking, served here on a gorgeous
terrace overlooking the Rizzanese Valley. All the dishes have been handed
down through generations and the ingredients come from the family farm.
Stay the night and enjoy Lily's home-
made fig jam at breakfast. €€

Filitosa

AUBERGE U MULINU
Pont de Calzola
Tel: 05 95 24 32 14
Wild river trout stuffed with local AOC
brocciu is the speciality of this highly
reputed *auberge*, housed in a converted
water mill on the banks of the Tar-
avo River. There are rooms available
if the wine list proves too much of a
temptation. €€

LE KIESALE
Pont de Calzola
*Tel: 04 95 24 35 81 or
04 95 24 36 30*
One of the island's finest wines, the
Domaine d'Abbatucci's award-winning
white, comes from this property, and
there's no better way of appreciating
it than over a wood-grilled fish supper at the homely little farm restaurant. €

Ajaccio

L'AQUARIUM
Rue des Halles
Tel: 04 95 21 11 21
Old established place tucked away
down a narrow alley behind the Place
du Marché. A dependable option for
inexpensive seafood, with especially
good fish soup and *friture du golfe*

(pot luck of pan-fried whitebait, cala-
mari and leftovers from the day's
catch). €

ARIADNE
Route des Sanguinaires
Bus No. 5 from Place De Gaulle.
Tel: 04 95 52 09 63
Lively beach bar-restaurant on the out-
skirts of town featuring an eclectic
mix of dishes from southeast Asia,
Africa, South America and the
Caribbean. Live World Music from
8.30pm most evenings. €

LE 20123
2 rue Roi-de-Rome
Tel: 04 95 21 50 05
Ajaccio's quirkiest Corsican speciality restaurant, decked out with old
village ephemera (including a 1960s
Vespa). The food is definitive mountain cuisine: top-grade *charcuterie*, excellent pork stews and chestnut-flour
desserts. €€

LE FLORIDE
Port de Plaisance Charles-d'Oornano
Tel: 04 95 22 67 48
The serious seafood lover's choice:
prime cuts of devil fish, snapper, mullet and bream, served in a smart dining hall fronting the posh end of the
marina. €€

The West Coast
Piana/Calanches

LES ROCHES ROUGES
On the Porto road
Tel: 04 95 27 81 81
If anywhere is likely to seduce you
into splurging on a *menu gas-
tronomique* it will be this elegant
restaurant, whose Art-Deco dining hall
exudes 1920s sophistication. Come
early for an *apéritif* on their superb
west-facing terrace, which affords peerless views of the Golfe de Porto. €€

Porto

LE SUD
Adjacent to the watchtower
Tel: 04 95 26 14 11
Stylish Mediterranean-fusion cuisine, drawing on North African and Spanish as well as Corsican influences: try the lamb tagine with almonds and apricots or pan-fried veal in orange, and be sure to book a seat on their wonderful *terasse panoramique* which surveys the marina and cliffs of Capo d'Orto. €€

Ota

CHEZ FÉLIX
Centre of the village, near the mairie
Tel: 04 95 26 12 42
Walkers with gargantuan appetites make up most of the clientele of this little village bar-restaurant, whose tiny terrace affords dizzying views across the Spelunca Valley. Local standards such as wild-boar stew and wood-grilled veal are prominent on a good-value *menu corse*, and there are usually couscous-based alternatives for vegetarians. €

Evisa

HOTEL DU CENTRE
Centre of the village
Tel: 04 95 26 20 92
You'll have to book days in advance to be sure of a table in this cosy mountain *auberge*, whose wild-boar steak in orange and dark chocolate sauce is the house speciality. For starters, they order in oysters fresh each day from the east-coast lagoons. No credit cards. €€

Galéria

STELLA MARINA
At the west edge of the bay
Tel: 04 95 62 00 03
Among the scattering of restaurants in the Balagne's most isolated resort, this is the most welcoming and dependable place to order local crayfish *(langouste)*, rounded off with their perenially popular apple pie flambéed in local *eau de vie*. €€

Calvi

L'ABRI COTIER
Rue Joffre
Tel: 04 95 65 12 76
Eating can be a pricey, hit-and-miss affair on Calvi's quai Landry, but here you're guaranteed value for money, plenty of choice and careful cooking, as well as optimal views of the marina. €€

CHEZ TAO'S
Rue St-Antoine, in the citadel
Tel: 04 95 65 00 73
Established by a White Russian deserter from the Bolshevik war in the Crimea (note the Rasputin-like photos in its vaulted interior), this place has been a legend since the 1930s. Film stars and pop idols flit through in summer for the cutting-edge nouvelle cuisine and bird's-eye views over the quay. €€

The sign of local produce

U FAMALE
Route de Porto
Tel: 04 95 65 18 82
Walk west of town towards the Punta della Revellata to find this refreshingly unpretentious Corsican speciality restaurant. Stock dishes include tasty lamb baked in *brocciu* and white wine, and moreish *fiadone* with *maquis* honey. Both feature on a copious set menu, and they also do less pricey pizzas. €

The Balagne
Calenzana
LE CALENZANA 'CHEZ MICHEL'
7 cours Blaise, opposite the church
Tel: 04 95 62 70 25
By far the best place to eat in the village, not least because of Michel's melt-in-the-mouth suckling lamb, served with wheat-rolled potatoes. And their wood-baked pizzas are delicious too. Popular with GR20 finishers, which ensures a lively atmosphere in season. €

Pigna
CASA MUSICALE
Tel: 04 95 61 77 31 or
04 95 61 76 57
Peerless panoramas over the olive groves of the Balagne coast and live Corsican folk music serve as a backdrop to the painstakingly traditional cuisine dished up in this ancient stone house on the edge of the village. Opt for half-board and you can breakfast on orange-blossom honey and chestnut biscuits. €€

Feliceto
OSTERIA U MULINU
On the Speloncato road
Tel: 04 95 61 73 23
Eccentric *ferme-auberge* in a converted olive-oil mill that's famous as much for the whip-cracking, gun-firing cabaret of its owner as for the top-quality food. Advance booking essential. €€

Speloncato
AUBERGE DE DOMALTO
6km (4 miles) below the village off the D71
Tel: 04 95 61 50 97
Superb *cuisine régionale* from the coast (sea bream in cream of lemon) and valleys (fragrant wild boar terrine), in a remote 18th-century *palazzo*. Tricky to located, but definitely worth the effort. €€

Pioggiola
AUBERGE L'AGHJOLA
Pioggiola
Tel: 04 95 61 90 48
Variously priced, superb value *menus fixes* featuring quails in cream of mint sauce and veal with wild forest mushrooms. On cooler evenings you can dine next to a blazing fire under exposed beams. €

L'Île Rousse
LES JARDINS D'EMMA
Col de Fogata, 2km (1 mile) along the Calvi road
Tel: 04 95 60 49 07
Refined *gastro-corse* menu with house specialities such as spider-crab soup, stuffed seafood and unashamedly decadent desserts, served al fresco in a flowery garden. €€

A TESA ('CHEZ MARYLENE SANTUCCI')
Lozari par Belgodère
Tel: 04 95 60 09 55
Acclaimed Corsican *ferme-auberge* ensconced amid *maquis profond* 6km (4 miles) inland from town in a converted riverside dairy. The Santucci family rustle up definitive Balagne dishes that include delicate courgette flower fritters and quails in honey. Everything comes from the garden or village farms, even the majority of the wines. €

Calendar of Special Events

There's no folk-dancing to be seen on Corsica any more. Centuries of oppression and suffering have removed it, along with the colourful costumes that one still sees on old etchings and postcards. A black dress for elderly ladies, and here and there a red sash with a corduroy jacket for men, might still just qualify as folkwear.

In contrast, another nearly extinct tradition has been revived in recent years: vocal polyphony, a musical form that had its heyday in the 16th century. It is an archaic form of singing whereby three basic voice-lines, known as *a secunda*, *u boldu* (or *u bassu*) and *a terza* blend together, each one relatively autonomous and reaching its own climax. This intense harmony is supposed to produce a so-called 'angel's voice', a line above the other three, which doesn't actually exist.

As recently as the 1980s anyone who wanted to hear this form of singing had to make the pilgrimage to various remote villages on religious festival days. There they would hear a handful of elderly local shepherds singing mass in the form of a *paghjella*. A *paghjella* invests even profane texts with a near-religious character, and is the island's common property, passed down through generations in verse form (usually two octameters). It is never written down,

but kept alive in melodic form, and often differs from valley to valley.

It is not only the politically active male-voice choirs eager to stress their 'corsitude' who add the *paghjella* to their repertoire: mixed and female groups have raised this form of unaccompanied singing to the status of an art form. Singers have now introduced it to the world at large: the Nouvelles Polyphonies Corses could be heard at the opening ceremony of the 1992 Winter Olympics at Albertville and the group Filetta have made a successful career recording film scores. Today it's no longer difficult to gain access to genuine Corsican musical tradition. An evening listening to a *paghjella* and also to simple monodic singing, such as the old *lamentu* (lament), must certainly number among the most vivid memories of a holiday on the island.

RELIGIOUS FESTIVALS

The religious year begins with **Epiphany** on 6 January. Special cakes can be bought at the local *boulangerie* or in the supermarket, into which a *fève* – either a large dried bean or a plastic symbol – has been baked. Whoever finds it in his piece of cake becomes the 'king' and is allowed to wear a golden paper crown. **Carnival**, unlike the event

Easter procession

in neighbouring Nice, is not a last chance for revelry before Lent, but is almost exclusively a children's festival and is sometimes even celebrated after Easter, as local timetables dictate.

As in other Mediterranean countries, **Easter Week** is of great importance. A series of sometimes quite dramatic acts of faith begins on **Palm Sunday**, or *palmiers*. Artistically plaited palm-tree leaves are brought into the church to be blessed, and are supposed to bring a whole year's peace to their households. Processional figures are removed from their various niches in the churches, and dressed in religious finery. Worshippers place lighted candles at their feet.

On **Good Friday** the male members of the religious fraternities, known as *confrèries*, carry the processional figures (which are enormously heavy and are sometimes in groups known as *chasses*) through the crowds of worshippers. In some towns – with particular fervour practised in Calvi – the procession of *confrèries* becomes a *granitula* or *girandula*, a kind of spiral that keeps forming and re-forming, like an archaic symbol of man's existence from embryo to death and then to rebirth.

Erbalunga at Cap Corse is renowned for its circular variation, known as *cerca*. In Bonifacio the itineraries of several *confrèries* cross at different times during the day, and in Corte a *Christ mort* gets carried through the streets at dusk. In Sartène thousands of people line the streets to watch a penitent known as the *catenacciu*, wrapped in a red cowl, shouldering a wooden cross and dragging a heavy chain, *a catena*, attached to his ankle. More and more towns on the island seem to be adopting this tradition – all that sunshine seems to produce quite a few 'sinners' these days.

The second major festival in the church year – apart from Ascension

– is the **Immaculate Conception** on 8 September. The statues of the Virgin are removed from the churches once again, and there is a particularly famous procession in the Niolo village of Casamaccioli *(see page 34)*. There's also a very colourful fair held there, which is known as **A Santa** for short. On **All Saints' Day** *(Toussaint)*, candles and huge chrysanthemum bushes are carried to the graveyards.

At **Advent** the churches start filling up with cribs, and in Bastia there's actually an **international crib show**. The habit of placing a Christmas tree in one's living-room is still not all that widespread on Corsica – though the supermarkets shower you for weeks on end with Bing Crosby, Ella Fitzgerald and various choirs. It's at Christmas time that the shelves in the shops here start to bend under the sheer weight of French specialities that the Corsicans usually have to do without. The highlight of **Christmas Eve** is the traditional *bûche*. It's actually the broadest part of a tree-trunk, which the menfolk saw down to size and which is then meant to crackle away in an open fireplace until everyone gets back from mass – but the *bûche* you find today is made of pastry, covered with various bits of decoration, and usually contains a sickly-sweet filling.

The big Christmas meal and the exchanging of presents take place on the **first day of Christmas** – there isn't a second one, the shops are already open again by then, just as they are late into Christmas Eve. **New Year's Eve** is the time for parties and balls, enlivened not only with fireworks and blank gun fire but often with real ammunition too.

SECULAR FESTIVALS

On the evenings of **Midsummer, Saint-Jean**, and the French national holiday on **14 July**, you will come across firework displays in the resort towns. At the end of the first week in July Bastia commemorates the succession (Le Relève) of the Genoese governor in an historical setting. In Ajaccio, Napoléon's birthday (15 August 1769) is very noisily celebrated.

The summer festivals begin with a lively **jazz festival** in Calvi in June. Immediately after it, and also in the Balagne, there is the **Festivoce**, a concert series in which local artists get together with performers from abroad. That's when the restored organs in the villages up in the mountains resound once more, when polyphonic harmonies are heard, and when *chiam'e rispondi*, a kind of mock-poetic question-and-answer game, gets recited off the cuff at Casamaccioli. In brief, the island's recently regained cultural self-confidence gets into its stride.

Other highlights are the **Rencontres Polyphoniques** in mid-September in Calvi, a **Classical Music Festival** in

early September in Bonifacio, and a British Film Festival in early October in Bastia. The **Mediterranean Culture Film Festival**, also in Bastia, is held in February. In the same month Calvi, almost deserted by the tourists so late in the year, stages its **Wind Festival**, and there's certainly enough wind around that late in the year. Kites fly high above the beach, hanggliders hover above the slopes, scientists give lectures, and every evening musical performances are greeted by stormy applause.

Alongside many other events – in summer the newspapers have page after page of information – the **Tour de Corse** is an established part of the annual calendar: at the beginning of May, rally drivers from several different countries roar their way around the twisting and narrow mountain roads between Ajaccio, Corte, Bastia and Calvi.

Rather more sedate are the sailing regattas held between the Côte d'Azur and Calvi, which use the island of Giraglia, with its lighthouse, as a turning-point.

Veteran sings his piece

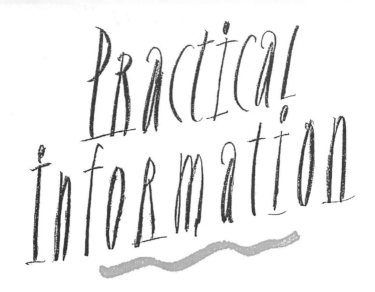

The ferry arrives

GETTING THERE

By Air

Air France (www.airfrance.fr) operate sdirect scheduled flights from Paris and Lyon to Ajaccio (Campo dell'Oro Airport), from Paris to Bastia (Poretta Airport) and Calvi (Sainte Cathérine/Santa Catalina Airport). More irregular but much less expensive connections are offered by the charter company Nouvelles Frontières (www.nouvelle-frontieres.fr). The Compagnie Corse Méditerranée (www.ccm-airlines.com) has regular connections from Marseille and Nice. If you're flying from the UK both British Airways (www.britishairways.com) and Air France operate daily scheduled flights from London Heathrow to Nice or Marseille. From there the Compagnie Corse Méditerranée (CCM, bookings through Air France /Air Inter) will carry

you on to the aforementioned island airports. The BA subsiduary, GB Airways (www.gbairways.com), flies weekly to Bastia. The onward flight will be with Compagnie Corse Méditerranée. Charter airlines offer direct flights from London and Manchester as well as from several cities in France and Western Europe to Ajaccio, Bastia or Calvi. There are also charter flights to Figari near Porto Vecchio. Departures from the UK are generally from Gatwick. You can book charter flights through www.holidayoptions.com or www.excelairways.com.

From the airports in Ajaccio and Bastia there are buses to take you to the city centres. In Calvi there are taxis.

By Sea

Ferries between the French mainland and Corsica, operated by SNCM (www.sncm.fr), are available the whole year round from Marseille and Nice to Ajaccio and Bastia, and also at least once a week from Nice to L'Île Rousse. During peak season there are also connections from Toulon on the mainland, and Calvi, Propriano and L'Île Rousse. From April to October there are speedboats (NGV = Navires à Grande Vitesse) from both SNCM and Corsica Ferries operating between Nice and Ajaccio, Bastia, L'Île Rousse and Calvi. For visitors who are departing from Italy, Corsica Ferries (www.corsicaferries.fr) sail regularly

The right footwear is important

between Livorno and Bastia, and during peak season there are also connections from Savona to Bastia and L'Île Rousse. MOBY lines departs from Genoa, Livorno and Piombino to Bastia, and offer through-tickets via Bonifacio to Santa Teresa-di-Gallura on the island of Sardinia. Corsica Marittima runs a number of boats from Genoa and Livorno to Bastia. There are also ferries operating between Santa Teresa-di-Galliura (on the island of Sardinia) and Bonifacio.

All ports of departure in France and Italy can be reached directly via motorway. As an alternative to driving your own car to the ferry terminal there are several SNCF motor-rail services that you might want to consider, not only those departing from Paris, but also the direct overnight connections between Calais and Nice, Boulogne and Livorno.

TRAVEL ESSENTIALS

When to Visit

The coastal resorts are packed from mid-July until the end of August. Visiting the island during these weeks can prove pretty tiresome, not least because it's so hot. The ideal time to travel would be from the end of May onwards, and then again after the first week in September. Before the peak holiday season the island is still green, and covered with flowers that fill the air with an incomparable scent. Napoleon is reputed to have said he could smell his native island before it came into view.

Until mid-May the climate is usually unpredictable, and from the beginning of October onwards there are quite a few showers. There again, the weather tends to stabilise nicely in November, and then stays mostly fine until Christmas. In January and February snow occasionally falls as low as the 500m (1,000ft) mark. High mountain passes can suddenly be closed by snowfalls as late as April.

Visas and Passports

Citizens of EU countries, and of Andorra, Cyprus, Iceland, Liechtenstein, Malta, Monaco, Norway, Switzerland, Canada and the United States do not need a visa to visit France. All other nationals should get in touch with the visa section of their local French Embassy or Consulate before travelling.

Clothing and Luggage

Remember if you're travelling around the island that temperatures can get pretty 'alpine' in the mountain villages. If you go hiking, even close to the coast, you'll need shoes with good grip because the paths are stony and there's quite a bit of loose rock about. Wearing a hat or headscarf as well as a strong sun-cream with a high protection factor is absolutely vital for those planning any kind of mountain tour, even in the cooler months. It is best not to brave the *maquis* in shorts as most of the smaller shrubs in this vegetation zone are thorny.

Modest attire (no shorts) are an absolute must for visiting churches, if you don't want to offend local sensibilities, and in remote villages you'll find that scanty clothing of any kind is widely disapproved of.

Electricity

The electrical current in Corsica is 220 volts. When using rather sensitive electrical appliances (such as radios, video cameras, etc.) bear in mind that the voltage is not as stable as it is on mainland France. Variations between 190 and 250 volts are perfectly possible. Don't forget to take an adaptor for any electrical appliance brought from home.

Time Zone

For most of the year, France is one hour ahead of Greenwich Mean Time, so if it is noon in Nice, it is 11am in London, 5am in New York and Toronto and 8pm in Melbourne.

Cargèse after much turmoil, nowadays about 8 percent of the population comprises migrant workers from former French North African states who come to Corsica as agricultural and construction workers. The immigrant population was also bolstered by the settlement of 17,000 Algerian-French between 1962 and 1966.

Government and Economy

Corsica belongs to France and, as has always been the case, French politics are decided upon in Paris. Corsican inhabitants have always felt that this is something of an affront and since the 1960s a regional movement has been increasingly involved in combating this particular situation. In 1975 Corsica's administration was divided into two *départements*: the Corse-du-Sud (Ajaccio Préfecture) and the Haute-Corse (Bastia Préfecture). Taken together these two *départements* make up the Région Corse (with its headquarters located in Ajaccio), which has been given a certain amount of authority in making governmental decisions. In 1982 Corsica received a statute of autonomy, granting it – in theory – extensive authority. In the wake of the outbreaks of violence and strikes in 1991 and subsequent elections in 1992, another even more extensive statute has been granted. But this certainly won't be the last step: for many Corsicans autonomy is not the same as independence.

GETTING ACQUAINTED

Geography

With an area of 8,800 sq. km (3,352 sq. miles), Corsica is the fourth-largest island in the Mediterranean, after Sicily, Sardinia and Cyprus. The island is 183km (115 miles) long from Cap Corse in the north to Capo Pertusato in the south. At its widest point it measures 83km (52 miles). The coastline measures 1,000km (625 miles). The island is basically a mountain range jutting out of the sea. With the exception of the coastal plains in the east, it is characterised by steep hills and mountains. Monte Cinto, at 2,706m (8,877ft), is the highest peak.

Population

Corsica has a population of about 260,000, of whom over 40 percent reside in the two principal towns of Ajaccio and Bastia. Members of old established Corsican families, who have lived on the island for centuries, still make up the majority of the residents, despite the emigrations. Ever since the Genoese first arrived, many young Corsicans have chosen to go to the mainland. Corsica also has a tradition of immigration: in addition to the Greek Orthodox refugees who finally settled in

The Moor with his headband

In 2003, a devolutionary package offering greater freedom from Paris was narrowly defeated in a referendum.

A good third of the gainfully employed population in Corsica is occupied in some sort of agricultural pursuit. Particularly in the east, there are large orchards of apples, cherries and plums. Large-scale irrigation has enabled the cultivation of citrus fruits. Olives and chestnuts are cultivated for local consumption. In the area around Porto Vecchio, cork production is also significant. High-quality wines are produced on Cap Corse (Rogliano), in the Nebbio (Patrimonio) and in the areas around Ajaccio, Sartène and Figari.

The most important source of revenue is tourism. A large portion of tourist-related businesses are operated by French people from the mainland or Algerian-French. With the exception of a few medium-sized businesses in Ajaccio and Bastia there is scarcely any industry to speak of. Coastal fishing does not contribute markedly to the economy.

Religion

The native population is almost without exception Roman Catholic. But mostly women are the regular church-goers. There is Sunday mass in the main towns, otherwise services are very irregular, administered by itinerant priests on certain days of the week.

MONEY MATTERS

The currency on Corsica is the Euro. There's a good exchange rate for travellers' cheques; if you exchange cash, though, you tend to lose out. Banks are open mornings and afternoons, except at weekends. Foreign currency exchange establishments stay open longer but often take much higher commissions or give you a less favourable rate than the main banks. MasterCard, Visa and American Express are the most commonly accepted credit cards; you can use them in all major hotels, restaurants, and also at service stations. There are cash dispensers outside most banks and major post offices.

Tipping

Most bills, when you get them, are presented in *servis compris* form, i.e. the tip is included. It's customary, though, to leave your waiter or waitress a tip of 10 percent or so, and taxi-drivers, too, expect you to round up the figure.

GETTING AROUND

By Car

Driving along the usually narrow, often confusing and badly surfaced roads is tiring and often dangerous. Corsicans tend to drive fast, without a care in the world – all those dents in their cars, and the various wrecked cars at the bottom of the island's ravines are proof enough. Don't hesitate to sound your horn loudly and regularly whenever you encounter a blind corner – mind you, it won't have any effect on cows or donkeys, who often choose just such places to graze. Fallen rock tends to remain where it is for ages, or it gets painted orange to warn drivers. Orange plastic tape is also used to warn drivers of other surprise hazards. Deep puddles in the road after heavy rain can also often force you to drive in the other lane. Don't expect to travel any faster than an average speed of 30 to 40 kph (around 20 mph) along the island's narrow twisting roads.

You may be surprised at the various ways of spelling place-names on maps and road signs. More and more parishes on the island are remembering their Corsican names, but no overall concept has been formulated as yet. The Italian suffix *-o* has been turned into a *-u* by the nationalists with a dot of white paint; several mayors place both versions above each other; others surprise everyone by using names that

The marina in Propriano

can't be found on any maps at all. Some place-name signs have been rendered completely illegible by nationalist graffiti or have simply been painted over altogether. I have taken account of this recent development in the itinerary descriptions.

There are hire cars available at all the island's airports, towns and larger tourist centres. The cheapest deals are to be found on the internet. However there are also cheap local rates available *(forfaits)*. Whatever you decide to do, it is highly advisable to take out comprehensive insurance on the car *(assurances)*.

By Train

Bastia, Calvi and L'Île Rousse are connected to Corte and Ajaccio via a narrow-gauge diesel railway line. The Corsicans refer to it as *u trinichellu* ('the little railway') and the French as *la Micheline*. There are between two and four connections daily in each direction; the trip from Bastia to Calvi takes 2 hours, and the one to Ajaccio around 3 hours. The Calvi-L'Île Rousse route operates more frequently from the end of June to the end of September and stops at the beaches if required. The trip

'La Micheline' at the station

across the alpine watershed from Ponte Leccia to Ajaccio is a real experience.

The Bastia–Biguglia route on the east coast, and the Calvi–L'Île Rousse one on the west coast are used more frequently because they are tramways.

By Bus

There are bus connections throughout the year between Bastia, Ponte Leccia, Corte and Ajaccio, Bastia and Porto-Vecchio, Bastia and L'Île Rousse/Calvi and Ajaccio, Cargèse, Porto, and – in peak season – between Saint-Florent and L'Île Rousse/Calvi.

Bus excursions are offered from all holiday centres in Corsica. Visitors who come to the island without their cars can discover some of the most beautiful scenery in Corsica by joining up with one or more of these relatively inexpensive bus tours.

By Bicycle and Boat

Cyclists can experience the varied landscape and vegetation contained in a small area more intensely than car passengers. Traffic is especially minimal along minor roads in the island's interior. A good map is indispensable for bike touring. It's also possible to rent bicycles in Corsica, particularly in the coastal resorts.

For those visitors wishing to get to know Corsica by boat, but who do not own their own ocean-going vessel, tour agencies offer a number of opportunities in the form of organised cruises or yacht voyages.

Boat excursions present an enjoyable and relatively inexpensive means by which to explore the Corsican coastline. All the following trips are possible: Ajaccio to the Iles Sanguinaires; Bonifacio to the Grotte du Sdragonato and other caves in the sea cliffs as well as to the islands of Lavezzi, Baïnzo and Cavallo; Calvi to Girolata; Saint-Florent to beaches in the Agriates region; and from Porto to the Calanches of Piana and Girolata.

Maps

A detailed pull-out map is included in the back of this guide. Corsica is also covered by the maps Carte Michelin 90, 1:200 000 and Carte IGN *(Institut Géographique National)* 116 Série Rouge 1:250 000.

The island is covered in two halves, at a scale of 1:50,000 by the IGN Série Verte maps 73 (north) and 74 (south) though this is very hard to get hold of these days, pending a reprint. For more detailed coverage, showing paths, etc, the IGN TOP aka 'Series Bleus' maps on a scale of 1:25 000 are recommended.

HOURS & HOLIDAYS

Opening Hours

Most shops open their doors between 9am and 10am in the morning, and bakeries open as early as 7am. They take a lunch break from noon till 3pm before finally closing at around 7pm. Variations of half an hour or so each way are quite common. These times apply all year round and include Saturday. In the peak season, supermarkets are open all day and often on Sunday mornings as well.

Public Holidays

1 January, Easter Sunday, Easter Monday, 1 May, 8 May (1945 Armistice Day), Ascension Day, Whit Monday, 14 July, 8 September (Assumption of the Virgin Mary), All Saints' Day, 11 November (1918 Armistice Day), and Christmas Day. Most offices and shops close on these days, but you will find the odd baker or shop open. If holidays fall on Thursday or Tuesday, banks and offices take an extra day off.

ACCOMMODATION

From early July until the end of August, accommodation on the island is extremely hard to find unless you've reserved in advance – even in the mountain villages. The best time to book for this period is around Easter or even before.

The local tourist information offices (Syndicats d'Initiative or Offices de Tourisme) keep useful lists of hotels and rental accommodation. To find out the prices you often have to go directly to the respective hotel or landlord.

Hotels

There are over 400 hotels on Corsica, most of them on the coast. The majority are 2-star. In the island's interior you'll often find rather basic 1-star establishments. If you reserve in advance, expect to be asked to make a deposit *(arrhes)*. The following is a selection of recommended hotels in and around the major centres covered in this guide:

All price codes refer to the cost of a double room. Credit cards are accepted unless otherwise stated.

€ = Budget: under €55
€€ = Moderate: €55–100
€€€ = Expensive: €100 and up

Bastia

CENTRAL
3 rue Miot
Tel: 04 95 31 71 12
www.centralhotel.fr
Bastia's most commendable budget option, occupying the first floor of an old tenement, a stone's throw from Place St-Nicholas. **€€**

POSTA-VECCHIA
Quai-des-Martyrs-de-la-Libération
Tel: 04 95 32 32 38
www.hotel-postavecchia.com
A choice of differently priced rooms next to the Vieux Port – the only hotel in this atmospheric area. **€**

LES VOYAGEURS
9 av Maréchal-Sébastiani
Tel: 04 95 34 90 80

The off-season

www.hotel-lesvoyageurs.com
Very smart, central and well placed for the ferry terminal, though lacking views. €€

L'ALIVI
3km (2 miles) north on the Route du Cap
Ville Pietrabugno
Tel: 04 95 55 00 00
www.hotel-alivi.com
Luxurious 3-star hotel on the city's northern fringe, with gloriously light, spacious rooms facing across the Ligurian Sea to the Tuscan Islands. €€€

PIETRACAP
Route de San Martino
Tel: 04 95 31 64 63
www.hotel-pietracap.com
This district's other chic 3-star hotel, close to L'Alivi, but higher up the hillside, with correspondingly more open views and attractive landscaped gardens. €€€

Cap Corse
Nonza

AUBERGE PATRIZI
Tel: 04 95 37 82 16
A scattering of old schist and granite houses, packed on to the steep hillside above Nonza beach. €€

Port Centuri

VIEUX MOULIN
Tel: 04 95 35 60 15
www.le-vieux-moulin.net
Former *maison d'Americain* overlooking the island's most picturesque fishing harbour. Worth staying here just to have the run of its lovely stone terrace. €€

Rogliano

AUBERGE SANT'AGNELLU
Tel: 04 95 35 40 59
www.hotel-usantagnellu.com

Former *Mairie* high above Macinaggio, converted into a welcoming, plush country inn that has more character than most, plus a quality restaurant. €€

Macinaggio

U RICORDU
on the south side of the route de Rogliano
Tel: 04 95 35 40 20
www.hotel-uricordu.com
The northern cape's swishest hotel, set back from the harbour front with its own pool and tennis court. €€

Erbalunga

CASTEL BRANDO
Tel: 04 95 30 10 30
www.castelbrando.com
Elegant 18th-century *maison d'Americain*, framed by palms and crammed with period furniture and engravings. One of Corsica's few genuine heritage hotels. €€€

San Martino di Lota

LA CORNICHE
San Martino di Lota
11km (7 miles) north of Bastia along the corniche road
Tel: 04 95 31 40 98
www.lacorniche.com
Modern Logis de France place high up on the corniche, whose rooms make the most of the panoramic views. €€

The Nebbio
St-Florent

MAXIME
Route d'Oletta, just off place des Portes
Tel: 04 95 37 05 30
This is a small, impeccably well maintained and modern place, hidden down a side road off the plane-shaded main square. €€

LA ROYA
Plage de la Roya
Tel: 04 95 37 00 40
www.hoteldelaroya.com
Self-consciously stylish 3-star hotel on the outskirts, next to the town beach, set in extensive gardens and with a gastronomic restaurant. €€€

Le Magnolia in Calvi

Check your locks

Castagniccia

Pedicroce

LE REFUGE
Tel: 04 95 35 82 65
Fax: 04 95 35 84 42
Castagniccia's only hotel clings to the steep valley side, surveying a vast spread of chestnut forest and hills. €

Corte and the Niolo

Corte

LA RESTONICA
2km (1 mile) south of Corte
Vallée de la Restonica
Tel: 04 95 45 25 25
www.aubergerestonica.com
Wood panels, leather furniture and hunting trophies define the character of this old-style mountain *auberge*, set up by a former football star. €€

DOMINIQUE COLONNA
2km (1 mile) south of Corte
Vallée de la Restonica
Tel: 04 95 45 25 65
www.dominique-colonna.com
Sister concern of La Restonica, in a more modern mould but at the same lovely location beside a mountain stream, surrounded by pine woods. €€

DU NORD ET DE L'EUROPE
22 cours Paoli
Tel: 04 95 46 00 33
www.hoteldunord-corte.com
Budget hotel in the heart of town that has retained its 19th-century charm without descending into shabbiness (as most of the competition has). Reception at the adjacent Café du Centre. €

Calacuccia

HOTEL DES TOURISTES
Tel: 04 95 48 00 04
Fax: 04 95 48 05 92
Large, no-frills place, little altered since its 1930s heyday, with rooms to suit most budgets and basic dorms for hikers. €

HOTEL L'ACQUA VIVA
Tel: 04 95 48 06 90
Fax: 04 95 48 08 82

Pleasant, mid-scale motel in a modern building at the foot of Monte Cinto. €€

Aléria/Cateraggio

L'ATRACHJATA
Tel: 04 95 57 03 93
Fax: 04 95 57 08 03
www.hotel-atrachjata.net
Plush 3-star hotel on the roadside. Hardly the most inspiring location, but comfortable enough and a convenient place to break a journey along the east coast. €€

Solenzara

MAQUIS ET MER
On the north side of the village
Tel: 04 95 57 42 37
Fax: 04 95 57 46 85
An elegant Riviera-style mansion dating from the 19th century, with traditionally furnished rooms and a serene poolside terrace. €€

Moriani

A CASA CORSA
6km (4 miles) south of Moriani, just north of the D71 junction on the highway
Tel: 04 95 38 01 40
Fax: 04 95 37 07 11
Friendly little B&B just off the main Bastia–Porto-Vecchio highway, with lovingly decorated rooms and a sunny breakfast terrace. €

The South

Porto-Vecchio

GOÉLAND
Port de Plaisance
Tel: 04 95 70 14 15
Fax: 04 95 72 05 18
Email: hotel-goeland@wanadoo.fr

Pleasantly old-fashioned place on the waterside below the citadel – no other hotel in town has such a desirable location. €€

MODERN

10 cours Napoléon
Tel: 04 95 70 06 36
Recently renovated hotel on the main square. Some of its rear-side rooms face the gulf. €€

PANORAMA

12 rue Jean-Nicoli
Tel: 04 95 70 07 96
Fax: 04 95 70 46 78
Basic *pension*-style hotel of a kind that's fast disappearing in Corsica, run by an elderly couple. Low tariffs are its main selling point, but the rooms are clean. €

GRAND HOTEL DE CALA ROSSA

Cala Rossa, 4km (2.5 miles) northeast of town, near Lecci di Porto-Vecchio
Tel: 04 95 71 69 24
www.cala-rossa.com
One of Corsica's finest hotels, screened by umbrella pines above its own beach. The driftwood decor and teak decks are delightful, the rooms light and private, and the restaurant Michelin-starred. €€€

Palombaggia

ROC E FIORI

Bocca dell Oro, 1km inland from Palombaggia beach
Tel: 04 95 70 45 20
Fax: 04 95 70 47 61
www.rocefiori.com
A cluster of exclusive suites and apartments, all painted in fresh Mediterranean pastels and set amid sea-facing, landscaped gardens. €€€

Bonifacio

CENTRE NAUTIQUE

The marina
Tel: 04 95 73 02 11
www.centre-nautique.com
Warm-toned wooden walls and nautical bits and bobs set the tone of this stylish hotel on the quayside. The rooms are on two storeys connected by spiral staircases. €€€

DES ÉTRANGERS

4 av Sylvère-Bohn
Tel: 04 95 73 01 09
Fax: 04 95 73 16 97
Bonifacio's only bona-fide budget hotel, on the main road out of town, has simply furnished double-glazed rooms. €€

A TRAMA

The Route de Santa Manza
Tel: 04 95 73 17 17
www.oda.fr/aa/trama
Secluded 3-star hotel, tucked away behind a wall of Mediterranean vegetation 1½ km out of town. Ranged around a pool and relaxing garden, the rooms all have private terraces. €€€

LE ROY D'ARAGON
13 quai J. Comparetti
Tel: 04 95 73 03 99
Fax: 04 95 73 07 94
Email: info@leroydaragon.fr
The least expensive option facing the marina, with all the usual trimmings of a three-star hotel and particularly good shoulder-season discounts. €€

Cala Longa

MARINA DI CAVU
6km (4 miles) east of
Bonifacio on the D258
Tel: 04 95 73 14 13
Fax: 04 95 73 04 82
www.marinadicavu.com
Swathed in flowering *maquis* on a slope looking out to the Îles Lavezzi, this isolated luxury hotel boasts a sublime pool and gourmet restaurant. €€€

Santa Manza

DU GOLFE
6km (4 miles) northeast
of Bonifacio on the D58
Tel: 04 95 73 05 91
www.corsud.com/golfe
Homely 2-star hotel perched on the edge of a secluded bay, with shuttered windows and a dependable restaurant on the ground floor. €€

Propriano

BELLEVUE
Av Napoléon
Tel: 04 95 76 01 86
Fax: 04 95 76 38 94
Friendly, inexpensive and perfectly placed opposite the quayside. Aask for a front-side room *(côté mer)* for the best of the views. €€

LOFT HOTEL
3 rue Capitaine Camille-Piétri
Tel: 04 95 76 17 48
Fax 04 95 76 22 04
Great-value rooms with minimalist modern decor in a converted warehouse, tucked away behind the seafront area. €

Sartène

ROSSI HOTEL (FIOR DI RIBA)
1km west of town on the Propriano road
Tel: 04 95 77 01 80

Fax: 04 95 73 46 67
Simple but smart family-run place looking across the Rizzanese Valley a short drive out of town. Has a small pool that's very welcome in summer. €€

Ajaccio

DU GOLFE
5 bd du Roi-Jérôme
Tel: 04 95 21 47 64
Fax: 04 95 21 71 05
www.hoteldugolfe.com
Comfortable 3-star hotel opposite the Place du Marché and ferry port. €€

KALLISTÉ
51 cours Napoléon
Tel: 04 95 51 34 45
Fax: 04 95 21 79 00
www.hotel-kalliste-ajaccio.com
Modern place occupying the third floor of an old Napoleon-era tenement on the main street, with ample off-road parking and a helpful English-speaking management. The best mid-range choice. €€

U SAN CARLU
8 bd Danielle-Casanova
Tel: 04 95 21 13 84
Fax: 04 95 21 09 99
At the top of this bracket, but easily the most appealing option in the Old Town, right opposite the Citadel and beach. Recommended for disabled travellers. €€

LA PINEDE
Route des Sanguinaires
Tel: 04 95 52 00 44
www.la-pinede.com
Swish 4-star hotel on the edge of town, commanding fabulous views over the gulf, with a pool and a clay tennis court. One of the few luxury places in Ajaccio that deserves its tariff. €€€

The West Coast
Cargèse

LES LENTISQUES
Plage de Pero
Tel: 04 95 26 42 34
Fax: 04 95 26 46 61
www.leslentisques.com

Refreshingly unpretentious 3-star hotel, right behind one of the west coast's most attractive beaches. Good low-season discounts. €€

Piana

LES ROCHES ROUGES
Tel: 04 95 27 81 81
Fax: 04 95 27 81 76
www.lesrochesrouges.com
Unquestionably the most romantic hotel on the island, dating from the early 20th century. Its views over the Golfe de Porto are sublime, and the 1920s Alpine-style architecture and Art Deco decor timelessly elegant. €€

Porto

LE GOLFE
Porto Marina
Tel: 04 95 26 13 33
Dependable budget hotel bang opposite the Genoese watchtower. All of the rooms are sea facing, which is a rarity in this price bracket. €

HOTEL LE COLOMBO
Porto marina
Tel: 04 95 26 19 90
www.porto-tourisme.com/colombo
A notch up in terms of comfort from Le

Golfe and decked out with driftwood sculpture and sea-blue paint. €€

Évisa

LA CHATAIGNERAIE
on the Porto road
Tel: 04 95 26 24 47
Well-kept en-suite rooms behind a traditional granite building, smothered in chestnut trees. Perfectly placed for valley walks, and the proprietress is American. €

Galéria

STELLA MARINA
Tel: 04 95 62 00 03
Fax: 04 95 64 02 29
www.hotel-stellamarina.com
Sunny rooms with good-sized balconies, set above a flower-filled garden overlooking the bay. €

Calvi

CYRNEA
Route de Bastia
Tel: 04 95 65 03 35
www.hotelcyrnea.com
Large modern hotel, which is a 20-minute walk from town but close to the quietest stretch of beach. Outstandingly good value for Calvi. €€

GRAND HOTEL
3 bd Wilson
Tel: 04 95 65 09 74
www.grand-hotel-calvi.com
Time-worn but characterful vestige of Calvi's pre-war *grande époque*, retaining original furniture, fittings and feel. €€

LA VILLA
Chemin de Notre-Dame-de-la-Serra
Tel: 04 95 65 10 10
www.hotel-lavilla.com
Calvi – if not Corsica's – top hotel: luxurious Mediterranean-fusion architecture complementing grandiose gulf views. €€€

The Balagne
Calenzana

BEL HORIZON
Tel: 04 95 62 71 72
Simple village hotel facing the church, popular mainly with hikers. €

An old apartment in Sartène

Fun on the beach

Ferme-Auberge A Flatta

Tel: 04 95 62 80 38
www.aflatta.com
Luxurious rooms with exposed wood beams, stone walls and chiffon drapes, perched on the side of a wild valley 3km (2 miles) outside Calenzana. €€

Pigna

Casa Musicale

Tel: 04 95 61 77 31
www.casa-musicale.org
Live traditional music and fine Corsican cooking are the main incentives to stay in this charming hotel, but its rooms – decorated in Mediterranean pastels – are like something off a film set. €€

Feliceto

Mare e Monti

Tel: 04 95 63 02 00
Fax: 04 95 63 02 01
Granite-floored *palazzo*, standing in the shade of old cedars, with antique furniture and fine valley vistas. €€

Speloncato

Spelunca

Tel: 04 95 61 50 38
Fax: 04 95 61 53 14
Old family-run hotel, occupying the former mansion of an 18th-century cardinal, just off the square of one of the Balagne's most photographed villages. €€

Pioggiola

Auberge l'Aghjola

Tel: 04 95 61 90 48
Fax: 04 95 61 92 99
A gem of a country *auberge*: traditional Corsican architecture, fine *cuisine du terroir* and a pool, at bargain rates. €

L'Île Rousse

Napoleon Bonaparte

3 place Paoli
Tel: 04 95 60 06 09
Fax: 04 95 60 11 51
Originally built in the 1700s, this grand old *palazzo* is now somewhat frayed around the edges and overpriced, but it oozes *fin-de-siècle* grandeur. €€€

Santa Maria

Route du Port
Tel: 04 95 63 05 05
www.hotelsantamaria.com
Recently refurbished 3 star hotel, near the eponymous red rocks and ferry dock, with beachside patios and access to a private cove. €€€

Rental Apartments

Villas and apartments are advertised in the papers at home. Otherwise they can be booked through the local tourist offices. Other options are *gîtes ruraux*, bungalows and private rooms *(chambres d'hôtes)*.

Camping

Corsica's wild, rugged scenery makes you want to pitch your tent anywhere you like – you're not allowed to, though, because of the danger of fire and other environmental damage. The choice of proper campsites, however, is huge. Some are close to villages, others high in the mountains. Even during peak season there's always room.

HEALTH & EMERGENCIES

Reciprocal agreements regarding medical protection exist between the different European Union countries. But even EU visitors may want to take out additional cover. Visitors from outside the EU should certainly make sure they have medical insurance. Most doctors in Corsica can speak at least a little English. The SAMU *(Service d'Aide Médicale Urgente)* is on hand in case of emergencies.

There are hospitals in Ajaccio and Bastia, another near Porto-Vecchio, and in Calvi an *Antenne médicale* is on hand.

The addresses of chemists open for emergency service nights and weekends *(Pharmacie d'urgence)* are posted in chemist shop windows. There are chemists in both Ajaccio and Bastia that remain open until 8pm during the summer tourist season.

Emergency Numbers

Emergency medical aid (& ambulance): 15
Police: 17
Fire Brigade: 18
Sea Rescue: 04 95 20 13 63
Emergency medical service can also be reached by calling the following numbers:
Ajaccio: SAMU. Tel: 04 95 29 90 90 or 04 95 59 11 11
Bastia: Centre Hospitalier Paese Nuovo. Tel: 04 95 59 68 00
Calvi: SAMU Antenne Médicale. Tel: 04 95 65 11 22
Corte: Hôpital Civil. Tel: 04 95 45 05 00
Porto Vecchio: SAMU. Tel: 04 95 70 01 01
Sartène: Hôpital Cacciabello. Tel: 04 95 77 95 00

Security and Crime

In the towns pick-pockets and purse-snatchers are at work and theft also occurs in more rural areas as well as on less busy beaches. Car thieves, who usually frequent the larger towns and coastal resorts, are quick and efficient.

Terrorism and Strikes

Visitors should not be alarmed by reports of terrorism. Attacks by heavily disguised commando squads on more or less illegally-built housing or against objects of speculation built at the islanders' expense tend to be limited to the winter season, when the buildings are standing empty. In late summer, however, forest fires can pose a threat to campsites. The strikes by French ferry and aircraft operators can also be unpleasant – they tend to take place unannounced in the period before peak season.

COMMUNICATIONS & NEWS

Post

Post offices *(Bureau de Poste)* in Corsica are open from 8am–noon and 3–6pm. The hours at smaller branch offices *(Agence Postale)* vary. Postcards and letters weighing up to 20 grams destined for other European Union countries are considered as domestic mail in terms of postage. Stamps may be purchased in the *bureaux de tabac* as well as from post offices.

Telephone

All telephone numbers in France have 10 digits. Paris and Ile de France numbers begin with 01, while the rest of France is divided into four zones: North West 02; North East 03; South East and Corsica 04; and South West 05. Freephone numbers begin with 08 00; 08 36 numbers are charged at premium rates, and 06 numbers are mobile phones.

To call Corsica from a foreign country dial 33 for France and 4 for Corsica, followed by the remaining eight digits. Few telephone boxes in France and Corsica now take coins, but some in bars and other public places do under the sign of 'Point Phone'. Most telephone kiosks *(cabines)* now accept telecards, available in post offices and tobacconists. To call other countries, first dial 00: Australia (61); Germany (49); Italy (39); UK (44); US and Canada (1). If using a US credit phone card, call the company's access number: AT&T, Tel: 00 00 11; MCI, Tel: 00 00 19; Sprint, Tel: 00 00 87.

The Media

There is only one daily newspaper which appears in Corsica: *Corse Matin*. The Corsican edition newspaper published on the French mainland *(Nice Matin)* contains several pages of regional and local information. In contrast to these are purely Corsican-nationalist magazines with some of their articles appearing in Corsican.

For most of the year, foreign magazines and newspapers are only available in the main towns and tourist centres, but in summer you can find them in almost every *Maison de la Presse*.

The six French television networks are in part privately and in part publicly operated. FR3 is a regional programme for Corsica. On the east coast Italian television stations can frequently be received. Now that satellite and digital TV have been introduced, international reception is extremely good.

NIGHTLIFE

The nightlife in the coastal resorts is rather limited as most socialising takes place in bars. The few discos are only really packed during the three summer months. In May, and in September too, these establishments are yawningly empty and extremely te-dious. During the rest of the year they only open their doors at weekends, or for the odd special occasion.

In season, things only begin to hot up quite late, usually around midnight, and then the fun lasts right through till dawn. The entry price (€15–20) to nightclubs usually includes your first drink – all the others after that cost a lot more. Sometimes posters promise some attraction or other, and dancing takes second place. Things really get going, though, once the young Italians are over for the summer. But even beach-bars which at lunchtimes are normally quiet, upright-looking establishments become transformed once evening comes around. Cocktails are served instead of salads, and quite often live music is put on to entertain you.

The so-called cabarets provide late-evening performances of good, old-fashioned folklore. Not a synthesizer in sight – here the performers plonk a stool under their leg to support the guitar and then deliver a whole series of nostalgic melodies, of the type Tino Rossi used to captivate Parisians with in the 1930s.

Finally, in July and August there are village fêtes held in central squares, where prices are very reasonable and visitors are welcome. Elderly couples can waltz and tango to their heart's content at these kind of functions, and even pop and disco-sounds have now made their entry on local scenes. But young people mostly find what they're

West coast sunset

looking for during their tourism apprenticeship down on the coast. Perhaps these hinterland evenings are the most Corsican of all, though: under the trees with their garlands of lights, hearing the owls hoot on your way home, and seeing an illuminated church-tower that stays in your m

Flora and Fauna

In the *Parc Naturel Régional de la Corse*, which covers the whole of the central mountain chain as well as the Castagniccia, there are still mouflons (a type of wild sheep), eagles and bearded vultures to be found, and in the Scandola maritime reserve several very rare species of bird, including ospreys, can still be seen flying around. Falcons and sparrowhawks circle above even the lowest of the mountain villages, and further up there are also goshawks and buzzards. The *maquis* contains wild boar, quail and partridge. There are no poisonous snakes on Corsica, though perhaps the odd miniature scorpion. The sheer amount of different species of butterfly is stunning. Orchids grow everywhere, including by the roadside; 300m (980ft) up, tiny cyclamen can be seen; even higher up you'll find white amaryllis. In the shallows of quiet bays you might be unlucky enough to tread on the poisonous

dorsal fin of a *vive* (John Dory) that has settled into the sand, and the spikes on the sea-urchins are almost as painful: they lurk just below the waterline on rocks.

Museums

The opening times of museums vary. Almost all of them are open in the morning 9am–noon, and then again in the afternoon 2–6pm. Some close on Sundays or for a few weeks in the winter. Museum admission is usually around €2–5.

Ajaccio

CHAPELLE IMPÉRIALE
The mausoleum of the imperial family, built in 1857 during Napoleon III's reign.
MUSÉE FESCH
In the main section between the chapel and the library. Italian masters dating from the 14th to 18th century.
BIBLIOTHEQUE FESCH
Also open on Friday evenings in the summer. In the left wing of the Palais Fesch. Impressive collection of old books. Founded by Napoleon's brother Lucien: as interior minister, he confiscated the books from monasteries and stately homes. Several fine exhibits.
MAISON BONAPARTE
One of France's national museums. No longer what it was, however, and not many of the exhibits are genuine.

One of many masterpieces at Musée Fesch

Exhibit from Aleria excavation

SALON NAPOLÉONIEN
In the Town Hall on the Place Foch. Paintings, busts, pictures and documents; copies of his birth certificate and death-mask.

A BANDERA
Rue Général Levie. Museum of Corsican military history.

CAPITELLU
Boulevard Danielle Casanova. History of the town and its population.

Aléria

MUSÉE JÉROME CARCOPINO
In the Fort de Matra. Prehistoric archaeological finds and also Greek, Roman, Etruscan and Carthaginian exhibits. The excavation site is open to the public.

Bastia

MUSÉE D'ETHNOGRAPHIE CORSE
Inside the former governor's palace, in the Citadel. Documentation of everyday, traditional life. Reminders of the fight for freedom under Paoli. Collection of amphorae.

Cervione

MUSEU ETNUGRAFICU
Behind the church, in the town hall. Local history museum for the Castagniccia and the Casinca regions.

Filitosa

STATION PRÉHISTORIQUE/
CENTRE DE DOCUMENTATION
Menhir statues and archaeological finds.

Levie

MUSÉE DE LA PRÉHISTOIRE
Archaeological finds from the primeval fortresses at Cucuruzzu and Capula. The exhibits include the island's oldest skeleton.

Morsiglia

MAISON NATALE DE PASCAL PAOLI
Birthplace of the 'Father of the Fatherland' in the Castagniccia. Mainly memorabilia. His tomb is located in the house chapel, next door.

Sartène

MUSÉE DE LA PRÉHISTOIRE CORSE
Menhirs, weapons, utensils and ceramics from the various archaeological sites in the region.

LANGUAGE

The official language on the island is French, usually spoken in the southern-French dialect (which is to say that most final consonants are pronounced). Corsicans also speak their own native tongue, both a spoken and written language in its own right and referred to as a *lingua nustrale*. This is a blend of Latin with some Italian and a little bit of French thrown in. In addition to these identifiable linguistic elements there are a number of other ancient, scarcely traceable sources, such as Iberian.

English is spoken by relatively few people on the island, mostly those engaged in the tourist trade

SPORT

Beach Life

Only a handful of frequently visited beaches close to the major centres of population maintain duty lifeguards. In bays that are enclosed by rocks dangerous currents can occur on windy days and these can easily pull swimmers out to sea. Offshore wind is less frequent, but it still poses risks for inexperienced surfers as well as for bathers floating on lilos.

Surfboards and catamarans can usually be hired in beach bars, and on the busier east coast you will find *pedalos* (pedal-boats) and even gondolas for hire. Here and there you can also hire extremely noisy water scooters.

Nude sunbathing is officially only allowed in certain club-villages, but is qui-

etly tolerated if undertaken at the far end of some beaches.

Children

Corsica is a great place to take children on holiday. They are welcomed everywhere and the water at most of the island's sandy beaches is quite shallow and the breakers fairly small. However, if you are taking children it's best to avoid the beaches along the rugged part of the west coast, where the water becomes deep quite suddenly and the undertow can be dangerous.

Golf

There are golf courses at Lucciana, near Bastia; at Punta di Spanu, near Lumio/Sant'Ambroggio; and in the Regino Valley near Monticello (both in Balagne); on the road to Bonifacio near Porto-Vecchio; and at Sperone, near Bonifacio. The latter is the only 18-hole-course, though the other clubs are planning to expand.

Riding

Horse and pony rides, charged by the hour, are available from various rental outlets near the coast. More rewarding, however, are day trips in the company of a guide along the old mule paths in the mountains. Here and there you can also hire donkeys or mules.

Angling

Sea-fishing on the beach is mostly unrestricted, apart from the odd stretch of coastline, but if you fish from a boat the local restrictions do apply. For the rivers and mountain streams you need to have a permit which is then valid for the entire island. Information is available from tourist offices, angling clubs, or the nearest town hall.

Diving

Snorkelling is rewarding wherever the water is clear, with a good mix of light sand and rocks beneath the surface. Diving proper tends mostly to occur on the rocky south and west coasts. Snorkellers can also try their luck at harpooning; anyone venturing out with oxygen tanks, though, won't even be allowed to keep a harpoon in the boat. Diving clubs are located at a number of centres around the island.

Hiking

The GR20 hiking trail runs along the alpine chain between Calenzana on the west coast and Conca, near Porto-Vecchio. It is a challenging undertaking and you should give yourself at least 10–11 days to cover the full distance of 175km (108 miles). Supplies can be replenished at most of the refuges punctuating the route, but outside the summer months bear in mind that these may be closed. Water is scarce on some stages: take advice from the refuge *gardiens* as to which springs are running, and always carry more than you think you'll need (at least three litres per person in warm weather). Sections of maps covering the entire route are featured in the

Where hikers can rest their limbs

French Hiking Federation (FFRP) *Topoguide GR20: A Travers La Montagne Corse*, available at most bookshops on the island.

The GR20 is regarded by French walkers as the country's toughest Grande Randonnée route and unless you're fit and properly equipped, you'll find it an arduous undertaking. To increase your chances of finishing, invest in dedicated mountain boots (2–3 season), a warm sleeping bag (3 season) and, above all, keep the weight of your pack down to a minimum (15kg/33lbs maximum for men; 10kg/22lbs for women).

The same applies to the less-challenging hiking trails that criss-cross the island at lower altitudes. Passing through villages, these wind between chains of immaculately maintained *gîtes d'étapes*, where you can enjoy the comfort of a clean hostel bed and cooked meal in the evening (advance reservations essential). Of course, this means it's possible to do without much of the gear you'd need on higher mountain routes such as the GR20, and you can thus walk unencumbered by a heavy pack.

There are currently five itineraries of varying lengths and degrees of difficulty. Second only to the GR20 in popularity, the **Tra Mare i Monti** starts in Calenzana near Calvi and makes its way in 10 spectacular stages to Cargèse on the west coast, via Girolata, Porto and several picturesque mountain villages. A shorter, but no less appealing option is the **Mare a Mare Sud**, in the far south between Propriano and Porto-Vecchio, which in five stages crosses an amazingly diverse array of landscapes, from dense deciduous forest to rocky uplands, with Pisan chapels and neolithic ruins to visit along the way.

Shorter day hikes are also featured throughout this book.

Cycling along Corsica's narrow roads

USEFUL ADDRESSES

Tourist Information

Information regarding Corsica can be obtained at the French tourist information offices located in your home country, at the Agence du Tourisme de la Corse in Ajaccio and at the various local tourist information centres situated throughout the island itself.

Corsica

Offices de Tourisme are located in the following:

Ajaccio: Place du Marché, Ajaccio. Tel: 04 95 51 53 03;
www.tourisme.fr/ajaccio
Bastia: Place St-Nicolas, 20200 Bastia. Tel: 04 95 55 96 96;
www.bastia-tourisme.com
Bonifacio: Rue des Deux-Moulins, 20169 Bonifacio. Tel: 04 95 73 11 88;
www.bonifacio.fr
Calvi: Port de Plaisance, 20260 Calvi. Tel: 04 95 65 16 67. www.tourisme.fr/calvi

Every city has a tourist train

Corte: Citadelle de Corte 20250, Corte.
Tel: 04 95 46 26 70;
www.corte-tourisme.com
Saint-Florent: B.P. 29, 20217 Saint-Florent. Tel: 04 95 37 06 04.
In addition to the aforementioned offices there are also tourist information centres (Syndicat d'Initiative) located at the most popular tourist centres.

France

Air France, 119 Champs Elysées, 75384 Paris, Cedex. Tel: 01 41 56 78 00; central reservation: 08 20 82 08 20; www.airfrance.fr
Nouvelles Frontières, central reservations: 08 03 33 33 33; www.nouvellesfrontieres.fr
Maison de la France, 20 Avenue de l'Opéra, 75041 Paris (no visitors), Tel: 01 42 96 70 00, fax: 01 42 96 70 71; www.franceguide.com

UK and Ireland

Air France, 10 Warwick Street – 1st Floor London W1R 5RA, reservations: 0845 0845 111. Dublin Airport, reservations 01 814 4060; www.airfrance.fr
French Government Tourist Office, 178 Piccadilly, London W1V 0AL. Tel: 09068 244123 (60p/minute), fax: 020 7493 6594;
e-mail: piccadilly@mdlf.demon. co.uk; www.france guide.com.

US and Canada

Air France, New York, 120 West 56th Street; Los Angeles, 725 South Figueroa Street, Suite 3251. Central reservation: 800 237 2747; www.airfrance.com
Montreal, Quebec, 200 Rue Mansfield, 15th floor, Montreal H3A 3A3.
Toronto, Ontario, 151 Bloor Street West, Suite 810. Central reservation: 800 667 2747.

Maison de la France/French Government Tourist Office, New York: 444 Madison Avenue, NY 10022. Tel: (212) 838 7800, fax: (212) 838 7855.
Los Angeles: Suite 715, 9454 Wilshire Boulevard, Beverly Hills, CA 90212-2967. Tel: (310) 271 6665, fax: (310) 276 2835.
Chicago: 676 North Michigan Avenue, Illinois 60611-2836. Tel: (312) 337 6339.
Miami: Suite 1750, 1 Biscayne Tower, 2 South Biscayne Boulevard, Florida 33131, tel: (305) 373 9177.
Montreal: 1981 McGill College, Tour Esso, Suite 490, H3A 2W9 Quebec. Tel: (514) 876 9881, fax: (514) 845 4868.
Toronto: Suite 2405, 1 Dundas Street West, M5G 1Z3 Ontario. Tel: (416) 593 4723.

Embassies and Consulates

American Embassy, 2 Avenue Gabriel, 75382 Paris, Cedex 08. Tel: 01 43 12 23 47 (information), 08 36 70 14 88 (visas); there is also a consulate in Nice at 31 Rue Maréchal Joffre, 06000 Nice. Tel: 04 93 88 89 55.

Australian Embassy, 4 Rue Jean-Rey, 75015 Paris. Tel: 01 40 59 33 00 (information), 01 40 59 33 06 (visas).
British Embassy, 35 Rue du Faubourg-St-Honoré, 75008 Paris. Tel: 01 44 51 31 00/01. There is a consulate in Nice at 12 Rue de France, 06000 Nice. Tel: 04 93 82 32 04.
Canadian Embassy, 35 Avenue Montaigne, 75008 Paris. Tel: 01 44 43 29 00.
Irish Embassy, 4 Rue Rude, 75016 Paris. Tel: 01 44 17 67 00.

FURTHER READING

Abram, David. *Trekking in Corsica* (Trailblazer, 2004). Corsica's long-distance hiking routes described and mapped in detail, with colour flora guide and hefty background sections.

Boswell, James. *An Account of Corsica* (contained in 'Boswell on the Grand Tour', Yale Editions, New York and London, 1955). Descriptions of Boswell's journey around the island and his visit to Pasquale Paoli.

Carrington, Dorothy. *Granite Island: a Portrait of Corsica* (Penguin paperback, New York and London, 1984). The most erudite and all-encompassing account of the island ever written, by the British expat aritocrat who rediscovered the Filitosa menhirs.

Carrington, Dorothy. *The Dream Hunters of Corsica* (Phoenix). An engaging exploration of Corsican occult traditions and folklore.

Elliot, Emma Eleanor. *The Life and Letters of Sir Gilbert Elliot* (London 1874). Compiled by the granddaughter of this aristocratic Scot, who as the Viceroy from 1794–96 acquired a love of the island and its inhabitants.

Lear, Edward. *Journal of a Landscape Painter in Corsica* (London, 1870). Through both his engravings and his writings, Lear was one of the first to portray the splendours of Corsica to the outside world.

Mérimée, Prosper. *Colomba* (Paris 1840). Based on the story of the vendetta that took place in the village of Fozzano in the Sartenais in 1833.

Schütz, Jutta (ed). *Insight Guide: Corsica* (APA, 2003). A comprehensive and richly illustrated guide to the island and its inhabitants, their history and their heroes.

Thresher, Peter Adam. *Pasquale Paoli: an Enlightened Hero* (London 1970). The most authoritative work on the island's greatest hero.

Vallance, Aylmer. *The Summer King* (London, 1956). Absorbing account of the fortunes of Theodor von Neuhof, the German nobleman who wanted to rule Corsica.

A pair of wild boars apparently two-stepping for tourists

Index

L–M

N–O

P

R–T

U–Z

ACKNOWLEDGMENTS

Photography **Alphons Schauseil** *and*
Page 5T **Leonora Ander**
81 **Anita Black**
2/3, 8/9, 10, 23, 40, 47, 58T, 74, **Pete Bennett**
76, 90, 92, 96, 97, 99B, 100, 104
98, 101 **Clare Griffiths**
13 **Historia Photo**
Page 5T **Hartmut Lücke**
1, 16, 28T, 29T, 31T, 32, **Neill Menneer**
36, 37, 38T, 41, 43, 45, 48, 49T, 51,
52, 54, 56, 57B, 64, 72, 83,
85, 86T, 87, 93, 95, back cover top
11, 12, 14B, 15, 47 **Jutta Schütz**
46, back cover bottom **Janos Stekovics**
27B **Werner Stuhler**
Front cover **Shaun Egan/Stone/Getty Images**
Cover Design **Klaus Geisler**
Cartography **Berndtson & Berndtson**